# Antsy Pants

## A Restless Pilgrim's Road to Santiago

### Amy Wiseman

**foreword by her dad**

*For my family*

# Contents

# Foreword

*Les Wiseman*

"Hey, dad, I am thinking about quitting my job and going over to France and then walking 800 kilometers across the north of Spain. It's called the Camino de Santiago. I will be gone for about six weeks". Not exactly what a parent expects to hear from their grown children. The first thing that came to mind was, *Ugh Millennials!* She suggested we watch the movie *The Way* to get a glimpse of what she'd be doing and where she'd be walking. The film follows a father who decides to walk the Camino in memory of his late son — a son who, it's worth noting, dies shortly after setting out on the very same journey. Not exactly inspiring confidence.

If you have had the pleasure of traveling, there is a sense of connectedness to that place when you see it again in a movie or on a page. You see yourself in that scene. There is some anecdotal evidence that connects you on a deeper level than just the visual. I have that privilege with the author of this memoir. She has brought the evidence of the Camino to our family. Not just the captivating visuals and stories that make for an experience that changes the trajectory of one's life but the essence of what a true pilgrimage is intended to be. You will discover in the following pages that a pilgrimage is not a place. It's what happens on the way there.

The psalmist David writes in Psalm 18:19 that "God brought me out into a spacious place; he rescued me because he delighted in me". (NIV)

Amy has done a masterful job in showing us that it isn't the space that rescues us, but the Creator of that space. Sometimes we need to be in a spacious place to hear His voice.

Enjoy,

Les

# Preface

I am, by nature, an antsy person.

Not in ways I'm always proud of. Restless where I should be settled, searching even in moments that deserve to be still. My mind runs ahead of my body, my body runs ahead of my plans, and my plans rarely survive contact with reality. I have started approximately forty-seven projects, finished several of them, and am currently in negotiations with myself about the rest. If there were a diagnosis for this particular brand of restlessness, I suspect it would simply read: *see title.*

What is the prescription for a restless spirit in a chaotic world? People will tell you breathwork, or cutting out caffeine, or finally committing to a morning routine. Maybe they're right. I have tried most of these. Cutting out caffeine was a dark time for everyone. But sometimes restlessness isn't a habit to be managed — it's a signal.

When your schedule and your relationships and your sense of direction have all been reshuffled, sometimes the only honest response is to follow that signal somewhere that looks, from the outside, a little dramatic. I walked 800 kilometers across Spain. On purpose. So take my advice accordingly.

Here's the thing about doing something that seems a little unhinged — it occasionally leads you somewhere true. I didn't know that going in. I thought I was looking for relief, the kind that comes from distance and movement and finally outrunning whatever had been nipping at my heels. I had a whole idea about what I was going to find out there. A plan, even. Which, if you've been paying attention, is already a bad sign.

I've spent four years turning over what happened on the Camino. Not because the experience was tidy (it wasn't) but because something shifted on that road that I haven't been able to unfeel since. The honest version of what shifted isn't particularly glamorous. Injuries happened. Weather was bad. Days stretched long with nothing to do but walk and think and occasionally question every decision that had led me to that particular hill. But there were also moments of unexpected beauty, remarkable kindness, holy disruption, and the strange intimacy that forms between strangers when you're all suffering in the same direction.

This is my story of becoming a pilgrim. It's not a guidebook — there are plenty of those, and I'm not qualified to write one. What I can offer is messier and more personal: my pain, my joys, my mistakes and my revelations. The word *pilgrim* is an old one, and it carries more weight than I expected when I first picked it up. Pilgrims aren't just people who walk a long way. Pilgrims are people who go somewhere on *purpose* — not just physical purpose, but the other kind. The kind you don't always have words for at the start. The kind that sometimes finds you before you find it.

Whatever brought you to this book — curiosity, your own restlessness, or someone who loves you and thought you needed a hint — I'm glad you're here. My hope is that something in these pages encourages you. My backup hope is that it makes you laugh. Either one counts as a win.

Let's walk.

# Glossary

- → *Buen Camino* [bwen ka-MEE-noh] - good way, good journey
- → *Ultreia* [ool-TRAY-ah] - Latin term meaning *beyond*
- → *Albergue* [ahl-BEHR-geh] - Camino-specific hostel
- → *Peregrino/a* [peh-reh-GREE-noh/nah] - Pilgrim male/female
- → *Municipal* [myoo-NISS-uh-puhl] - a hostel run by the town
- → *Pensión* [pehn-SYOHN] - small family run hotel
- → **Abuelo** [ah-BWAY-loh] - Grandfather
- → *Jamón* [hah-MOHN] - a dried, cured ham
- → *Paella* [pah-EH-ya] - a saffron-infused rice dish typically consisting of seafood, meat and vegetables
- → *Bocadillo* [boh-kah-DEE-yoh] - a baguette sandwich with jamon or chorizo and if you're lucky some tomato and a bit of olive oil
- → *Stroopwafel* [STROPE-vah-fuhl] - a traditional Dutch waffle treat filled with syrup or caramel
- → *Hospitalero* [ohs-pee-tah-LEH-roh] - A volunteer host
- → *Donativo* [doh-nah-TEE-boh] - donation
- → *Botafumeiro* [boh-tah-foo-MAY-roh] - smoke expeller, a censor used in Mass in Santiago de Compostela
- → *Siesta* [si-ES-tuh] - a short afternoon nap usually taken between 2 and 5pm

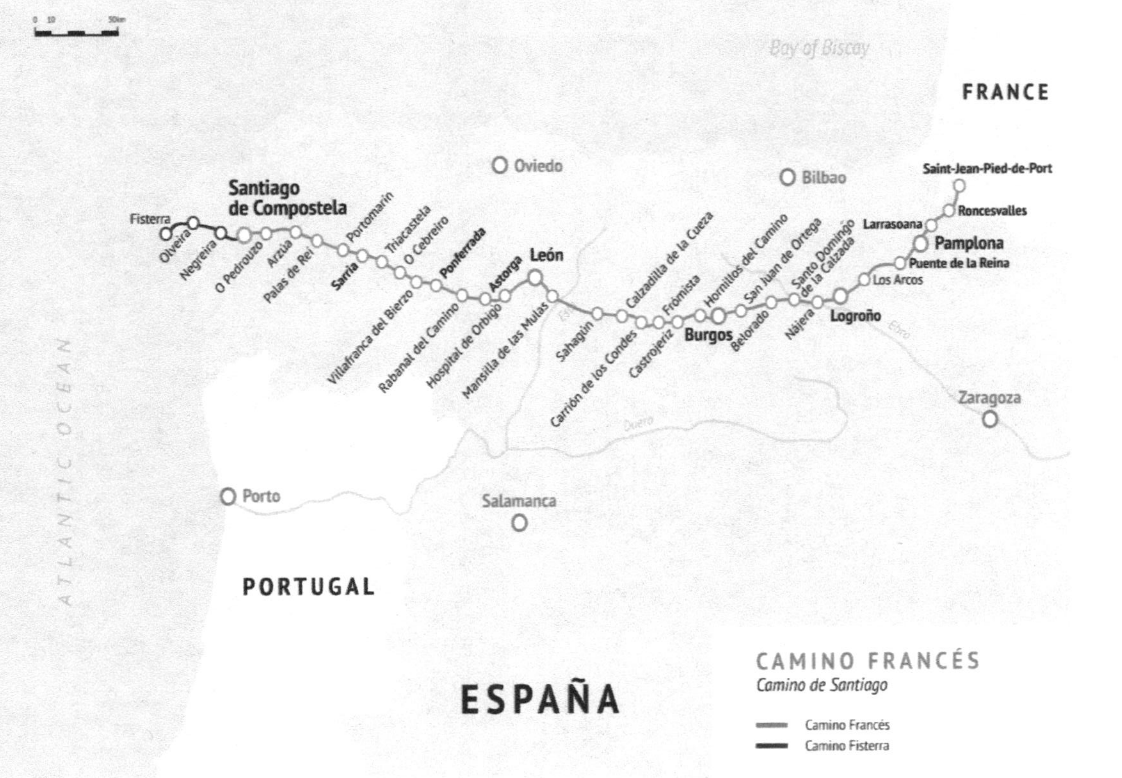
FRANCE
Bay of Biscay
Saint-Jean-Pied-de-Port
Roncesvalles
Larrasoaña
Pamplona
Puente de la Reina
Los Arcos
Logroño
Nájera
Santo Domingo de la Calzada
Belorado
San Juan de Ortega
Hornillos del Camino
Burgos
Frómista
Castrojeriz
Calzadilla de la Cueza
Carrión de los Condes
Sahagún
Bilbao
Oviedo
León
Astorga
Mansilla de las Mulas
Hospital de Orbigo
Rabanal del Camino
Ponferrada
Villafranca del Bierzo
O Cebreiro
Triacastela
Sarria
Portomarín
Palas de Rei
Arzúa
O Pedrouzo
Negreira
Olveira
Fisterra
Santiago de Compostela
Zaragoza
Salamanca
Porto
ATLANTIC OCEAN
PORTUGAL
ESPAÑA
CAMINO FRANCÉS
Camino de Santiago
Camino Francés
Camino Fisterra
0  10        50km

# 1

# Ultreia

*This is the stupidest thing I've ever done,* I thought as I trudged up the steep leaf-clad hill. The heavy rain from the morning weighed down my already dense backpack, and a fresh coat of sweat was all that I needed to convince myself that this trip was absolutely crazy. I had started on the trail before the sun rose, with a headlamp and a can-do attitude that died soon after encountering the first scarped climb. The morning had been beautiful. Before the rain started, I watched the sun rise over the misty hills and listened to the birds wake up. Picturesque. Serene.

I wasn't sure how early to start moving. I barely slept, keeping one eye on the other pilgrims in the room, not out of suspicion, just wondering who would be the first to get going. There was movement just before 6 a.m., and that is when I got up. I gathered my sleeping bag and gear and took them into the empty hallway, where I packed them up and put on my layers for the day.

I went up the dark stairs and opened the kitchen door to find the lights on and several other pilgrims dressed and getting ready to start walking. Some were eating a small breakfast or brewing tea; others were scribbling in their journals. Each time someone left the room, the others quietly wished them a "Buen Camino" and gave friendly nods - the traditional exchange between pilgrims on the trail.

I finished a cup of tea, hoisted up my pack and headed towards the door, eagerly listening for my own quiet send-off from the other early risers. When it came, I smiled and stepped onto the dark streets of St. Jean Pied-de-Port.

The day before, I had arrived at St. Jean just before noon. Rain fell throughout the morning; heavy clouds loomed. The mist didn't help the overall mysterious feeling this day held. Buildings shrouded in fog and the silhouettes of mountains teased the imagination. A habit of mine that seems to travel with me, wherever I go, is forgetting a meal or two on my first day of a journey. My stomach started growling after eating half a stale croissant in Bayonne. A cafe with older gentlemen playing cards near the entrance caught my eye. I ordered a coffee and a pastry and pulled out my guidebook to pass the time until the pilgrim office opened.

I entered the office excited and a little jittery (probably from the coffee). While waiting for my turn to get my pilgrim passport and maps, I spotted a bucket filled with shells. The scallop shell is the symbol of the Camino, and pilgrims tie them to their packs or walking sticks, branding themselves as travelers of the Way. I grabbed the first one I saw and immediately tied it to my pack.

The street filled with more and more pilgrims as the day went on, and I found myself not looking at the town anymore, but at the people instead. I had read so much about the connections you make with others on this pilgrimage, and I wanted to dive into the deep. I stopped at an outfitter close to the pilgrims' office to pick up some walking poles and spy on the others getting last-minute equipment. *Gosh, this makes me sound so nosy.*

Before checking into my albergue (pilgrim hostel), I climbed the tall, sharp steps to Le Citadelle, which, by the way, is a mistake when you've only had coffee and a bit of pastry. It is a great view, though. I looked down at the streets, trying to see if I could spot the route I'd be taking the following day. The fog was too heavy, so I let the coming day live in some mystery until I stepped into it.

***

Now, stepping onto the trail in earnest, I turned on my headlamp and followed the brass arrows and shell trail markers leading me to the Valcarlos Route. As it was still technically winter, the more exposed Napoleon Route over the top of the mountains was closed. Leaving town and heading into the surrounding farmland was exhilarating, despite the hour. I was alone!

Most people might find that terrifying, and maybe I should have. But I didn't. I was on a scavenger hunt! It was dark, and the rain made the path muddy, but I preferred that to walking on the verge of the road with the ever existing fear of traffic whipping around the many blind corners. As I walked, I kept my eyes peeled looking for the trail markers - either the Camino scallop shell or small red and white hiking trail markers - to ensure I didn't stray down one of the many intersecting paths or roads. It was quiet except for the sound of rain falling on the gathered trees next to the trail. So peaceful.

*Annnd now I'm out of water. Perfect. Why didn't you stop for more at the last town you walked through, you idiot? This is humiliating! It's my first day on the Camino Francés, and I'm dehydrated and alone in the woods. I have never felt so unfit in my life! Ill prepared...haven't stopped for a toilet...ugh.*

The woods had been enchanting...at first. The twists in the trail promised a beautiful dew-covered discovery at every turn. Until those turns inclined. The rain didn't bother me too much either. Until it started to pour.

It was raining most of the time, and those who know me well know I LOVE the rain. Anything that makes me feel like I'm in a Jane Austen novel, I'm all for it.

It's not as romantic as it sounds in "Sense and Sensibility".

I passed a couple of towns still walking up and as much as I wanted a hot cup of coffee; I decided to treat myself to that once I had made it to my day's destination of Roncesvalles. I had brought granola bars and one water bottle with me for the day. The granola bars were good and filling enough, and I felt I still had a good amount of energy. When I finally got to the last third of the walk, that's when I struggled. The beautiful wooded trails I was so looking forward to had become a cruel, steady climb designed to kill me. It is a twenty-five kilometer walk from St. Jean to Roncesvalles, and I felt as though I was walking fifty.

I looked around and saw people I had overtaken earlier in the day passing me along the trail, smiling politely as I wheezily nodded. I had heard that this pilgrimage was magical. There were miracles and provisions to be found all along the road to Santiago de Compostela. Maybe it was too much to ask for on the first day. *Maybe true pilgrims are the only ones who experience those miracles.* Finding a somewhat dry-looking rock, I sat down for the first time that day and surveyed my surroundings. *I am crossing the Pyrenees.* What a surreal thought! A pleasant distraction from the fact that I wasn't doing a very good job of it. I turned my head to the trail ahead and groaned. Another steep climb. I moved some frizzy and matted hair from my face and closed my eyes for a moment. *Just keep going. Just keep going. How long would it take me to sit here and collect enough rainwater to drink? Can I drink rainwater? No! No, Amy! Just get up and keep walking.* I slowly stood and continued to trudge through the forest.

There was a group of Korean ladies who had stayed in the same albergue as me the night before. During the main arduous climb of the day, we took turns passing each other. They didn't speak English but communicated with kind smiles and greeting gestures. One lady in the group saw me struggling and left clementines on fences and rocks for me as I sauntered up the trail. I happily took the fruit and savored each bite as if I had never eaten such a delicacy before. At one point, this sweet angel poured water from her own bottle into my empty one. I almost cried.

Soon after that, we found a water fountain and cheered! Roncesvalles wasn't far beyond that point, and I couldn't wait to arrive. I saw the top of the monastery in the distance and quickened my pace to the haven.

Albergue Real Colegiata. A monastery that has been in operation since 1127. That's a fact that I don't think ever really sunk in while I was there. Probably because the building has been renovated with modern amenities for today's pilgrims. There would be a few times on this journey where the awe of my surroundings came second to my desire for a chair. This was one of those times.

I pushed open the heavy door of the large building and found myself surrounded by volunteers armed with towels and teacups. Immediately, someone took my backpack and ushered me to a bench with the pilgrim paperwork on the table. An elderly man with biscuits and a steaming cup of tea in hand stopped me from taking the forms.

"Now, miss," he said as he slid the plate of goodies towards me. "All that paperwork can wait. I've got these biscuits for you, and I don't want you to move until they're gone."

This was so unexpected and kind; I didn't know how to take it in. He sat next to me on the bench and asked me my name and where I was from. He offered me more tea and biscuits, even though I hadn't finished the first round. I sipped my tea and looked around the room as more pilgrims made their way through the door. I watched their faces as they, like me, were greeted with warmth and treats.

After checking in, I went upstairs to find my bed and change out of my wet clothes. The beds were semi-private bunks that lined a long corridor. There were cupboards at the end of each bunk to house backpacks and gear. Many albergues do not allow boots past a certain point to keep the sleeping quarters sanitary and prevent them from smelling like a locker room. I rolled out my sleeping bag and headed for the showers.

Coffee was the next thing I was looking for, but I was impatient and settled for a cup of hot chocolate from a vending machine. Dinner wasn't for another hour or two, so I sat with my warm drink in the common room and checked in with my family. I wasn't there long before another pilgrim joined me. He was an Englishman who had arrived at the albergue around the same time I had. His name was Dan and, with very little to no small talk, he invited me to join him and a few others for a drink before dinner.

The restaurant was empty except for our small group of about six. The youngest in our party was fifteen-year-old Leo from Australia. He was walking the Camino with his dad, James, for the second time! The rest were first-time pilgrims from Poland, France and the U.K.

After drinks with our new friends, Dan and I made our way into a room with a long dining table. The room was filling up with our dinner group, and lively chatter carried throughout the space. I was thankful for the growing noise as my stomach was trying to match pitch in its attempt to remind me of how little I had eaten that day.

I was nervous about the dinner. Shortly before leaving for the Camino, I found out I had a gluten and dairy intolerance and needed to limit my intake. I felt anxious each time I entered a restaurant, wondering if they'd have anything for me and if I'd be brave enough to ask. Nine times out of ten, my imminent gut discomfort would ultimately take a backseat to my fear of inconveniencing someone with my dietary needs. *I did eat those biscuits earlier...* I had heard the phrase, "the Camino provides" a few times, but I wasn't quite ready to believe that it pertained to food intolerance.

Around the table sat pilgrims from all over Europe, the U.K., the U.S. and Canada. I breathed a sigh of relief as I heard someone from the other side of the table ask about gluten-free options. *Hallelujah! I don't care what it is; I'm going to get the same thing as he does.* The dinner was warm and delicious. Soup, fish with gluten-free bread, and a surplus of wine. We all started out as strangers, but as the hours passed, we became bonded by that table.

That was the night my Camino family was born.

Here's the thing: a kind smile would have been enough. A bench would have sufficed. A 'hello' was welcome but unnecessary. It was more than I needed. And it was beautiful. That will be a theme throughout this book. Ultreia is a word pilgrims will see and hear on the Camino de Santiago. In Latin, it means *beyond.*

2

# Welcome to Narnia

Everyone's faces were glued to the windows that morning. The world had gone white. It was still too early to see just how much snow had fallen during the night, but it was enough to set the place abuzz. There were some panicked pilgrims, some uneasy, some curious, and some who seemed unbothered by the change in the weather. And then there were some, like me, who were excited.

I am a Canadian-born, Michigan-raised woman who has had her fair share of experience with winter. Both good and bad. But this snowfall was magical to me! Accustomed as I was to snow, I felt giddy. Perhaps the Gregorian chants playing through the dormitories that morning contributed to this feeling. Or the fact that it was April Fools Day and we'd all woken up to a blizzard.

I got dressed in several layers and cut some thumb holes in my fleece pullover as I didn't have any gloves. The possibility of snow hadn't crossed my mind when I was packing for this trip. I had brought a fairly limited wardrobe of a rain coat and pants, lightweight hiking pants, two pairs of leggings, three shirts, a fleece pullover, and a week's worth of socks and underwear. My yellow backpack was on the smaller side, as I didn't want to tempt myself with packing too much.

Determined to start the day off right, I stepped onto the trail with my headphones on and worship music playing.

Music is so powerful. The only music I had listened to the day before were songs of self-deprecation I had made up in my head as I trudged through the forest. I mumbled my own miserable lyrics to a tune that deserved better, a self-pitying soundtrack for my slow, breathless climb. Those songs did little to motivate me, and I would not let that happen again. This day I was going to listen to music that would take the focus off of me, so worship music it was.

My favorite worship song is "Captivated" by Shawn McDonald. It has been for many years. A song describing God's fingerprints on every part of creation. These were the words that I wanted swimming through my mind on this day.

The daylight was growing brighter, and as I hiked through the ever-thickening snow, I found myself completely enchanted by the sparkling forest and the wind dancing off the hills. I had left the Camino and found myself in Narnia! I half expected the pilgrims that passed me would be the Pevensies in their fur coats looking for Mr. Tumnus.

The mountains that had caused me such grief the day before looked fresh and bright. Everything around me breathed newness. Snow covered the trail markers, which displayed the bright yellow and blue Camino shell, and although I knew the blizzard would continue throughout the day, I brushed the snow off the concrete columns so my fellow pilgrims wouldn't miss them.

The songs of praise that began my day lifted my mood, and now, engulfed in a snow-kissed wonderland,

I felt overwhelmed with gratitude for the gift of this place. As I walked, the snow weighed my boots down, and having learned my lesson from the previous day, knew that I had to listen a little closer to my body and take a break or two. I brought more water with me and found a canopy of trees to rest under. I stopped two or three times throughout the day to refuel. The snow was wet and heavy, but I felt lighter!

This was what I was hoping the Camino would be: hope-filled wonder and a feeling of renewal. I came here wanting so badly to enjoy time with God and to find joy in life again. This was a really good day, and despite my optimism, I would need to look back on it often to help me recall the ease with which I praised God. But it is easy to praise God when everything is beautiful, right?

Maybe it was magical because it was unfamiliar. As mentioned earlier, I am no stranger to snow, but here, I reveled in it. In the afternoon, the sun came out just in time for me to step carefully over glistening river rocks. The extra light gave me an incredible energy boost. I pictured myself as Bear Grylls, surviving and thriving in the harsh elements. *I'm basically a wilderness expert now.* Even though I knew I looked nothing like him in my attempts at stealth, my imagination was already on the run. While hopping across the rocks, I came upon my new friend, Dan, whom I had met the night before. We enjoyed chatting about our homes and families while occasionally helping each other over the more uneven parts of the path.

Though the glimpses of bright sun, good company, and beauty of the day were uplifting, it was still snowy and cold, and I fantasized about soup in the last leg of the day's walk. Thankfully, we didn't have far to go, and my steps became more determined when the rooftops of Zubiri came into view.

Our albergue was much smaller than the large monastery of Roncesvalles, but conveniently located a stone's throw from cafes and the church. Dan and I unloaded our gear and went in search of food. Finding a small restaurant, we walked in to find many of our new friends from dinner the night before. I ordered some soup, chicken, and wine. My face was still cold from the day's walk, so I leaned forward to let the steam of my soup warm my cheeks. *This is exactly what I needed.*

Whenever a new person walked through the doors of the pub, Dan would suggest pushing more tables together, regardless of whether he had previously met the incoming diners. He was wonderfully social, and sometimes I could imagine him welcoming new friends like the jolly spirit from "A Christmas Carol", "Come in and know me better, man!" (minus the robe, beard, and wreath, of course).

We all enjoyed drinks and talked about the snow. I don't remember anyone mentioning what they did for a living, which made me happy. Not because I was unemployed, but because it feels like a shortcut to getting to know someone. It provides a box for us to put one another in and, thankfully, experiences like these have no place for boxes. We would talk about where we were from and why we had decided to walk the Camino.

There are many chances for you to meet people on this trek, and it's strangely easy to talk to them. You see their shell, backpack, or slight limp and immediately know that you're in the presence of another pilgrim. The ease of conversation begins with the shared experience of the day, and then genuine curiosity kicks in and predictable small-talk forgotten.

As I sat among my fellow pilgrims at that pub, the warmth of the room and the hum of conversation wrapping around me, my mind would jump to months before when I would hide in the bathroom at work for a moment's peace. *How did I let it get that bad?* I'd lock the door, lean against the cool tile wall, and just breathe—trying to find five minutes where no one needed anything from me. For the past two years, working retail through a pandemic, I had been surrounded by others, and I unintentionally soaked up their issues and emotions like a sponge. The anger, the fear, the loneliness, the exhaustion—all of it pooled in me until I didn't know where their feelings ended and mine began. I didn't want to. I just didn't know where to put this ever-growing burden of being available to everyone all the time.

My younger sister, Kelly, suggested counseling to me after seeing me strangled by my work environment and stressful schedule. I'll always be grateful to her for that. Weekly sessions with a therapist helped my scrambling slowly begin to unwind. I finally had someone to help me unpack what I was carrying and to affirm that it was time for change. Someone who could say, "You're not broken. You're just carrying too much."

I needed a different job, a different atmosphere, and a different perspective. Here I was in a different crowd. The pub was alive with laughter and clinking glasses, snow melting off boots, faces flushed from wine and the day's cold. We had all lived through the difficulties of the pandemic, but we weren't here to wallow in our shared grievances. We were here just to be here. *Just to be.* I had forgotten that most people were isolated and hadn't been over-socialized like I was in retail. They had been starved for connection while I had been drowning in it. They missed people.

One of my assignments from my therapist was to set a timer for ten minutes and to write what I would want for my "best possible self". I remember sitting at my kitchen table, staring at the blank page, wondering if I even knew who that person was anymore. After completing the exercise, the overarching theme was people. Not fewer people, better interactions with people. Meaningful connection. Laughter that didn't feel forced. Conversations that went deeper than complaints about inventory and mask mandates. I wanted to like people again. And here I was, only on my second day on the Camino, surrounded by people, and loving it. *I'm actually loving it.*

I connected with Emilija from Lithuania and Gosia from Poland. These were two women I had seen on the trail throughout the day but didn't really meet until that night. Emilija had this bright laugh and disarming humor, and Gosia had a quiet warmth about her, the kind that made you want to sit closer. I had missed Mass the night before and jumped at the chance when Gosia invited Emilija and me to join her for the service happening in an hour. I am not Catholic, but my desire to attend Mass was twofold. First, I wanted to experience as much of the culture here as I could, to soak in everything this place offered. Second, I found myself dissatisfied with church as I knew it and longed for some new (or at least new to me) ways of connecting with God. Maybe the ritual and tradition would speak to something in me that contemporary worship hadn't touched in a while.

The three of us bundled up and walked to the Iglesia de San Esteban together, our breath visible in the cold air, boots crunching on the icy cobblestones. The street was quiet - the quiet that only comes after snow. We reached the church only to find the gate locked and no one around. We stood there for a moment, peering through the iron bars at the dark entrance, as if willing someone to appear. Later, someone informed us that the church's hours varied, and there would be no evening mass.

A little discouraged, we headed to a nearby coffee shop for lattes and chocolate bars. The cafe was small and cozy, with condensation fogging the windows, the espresso machine hissing in the background. This was a small thing, but that's what made it wonderful. *When did I stop appreciating the small things?* Our plans didn't pan out, so we opted for enjoying a sweet treat in each other's company instead of moping. We sat in a worn booth, wrapping our hands around warm mugs, talking about nothing and everything—our families, our reasons for walking, the way the snow had transformed the trail into something otherworldly.

Feeling quite content, we headed back to our albergue, our steps slower now, reluctant to let the evening end. After a full day of whimsical weather and joyous company, I climbed into my bunk and fell asleep thinking of all the magic that was to come the next day.

# 3

# **Heavy Boots**

I have done a couple of social media fasts, and it's incredible what it does for my mood by eliminating the noise for a while. My Instagram account was deleted before the Camino, and I wasn't sure about reactivating it. I needed some quiet. I had become numb to my surroundings and, essentially, my own health with the onslaught of opinions from my workplace, the news, the internet, and even friends. It amazes me how quickly one word can shape our emotions if we're not careful. Walking into Pamplona, I wasn't being careful.

The day started out with me realizing that the clothes I had "washed" (showered in) the night before were still damp. The shower method was one I had read about in some Camino blogs before the trip and was supposed to aid in saving money and time. This would be the one and only time I would try it. I refused to let it get me down. I wrapped my damp clothes in a plastic bag, put them in my backpack, changed into my spare clothes, and planned to do laundry that night.

I left Zubiri early with Emilija, and we walked together for the first little while, and then I found myself slowing down. The beautiful snow was melting, and although my boots had been triple waterproofed (thanks, Dad), I had stepped in some deep slush and now had soaking wet socks. *That's not great, but I can change my socks next time I find a bathroom or somewhere to stop.* I would have to walk for a long time before I found a dry place to sit.

The heavy snow weighed down the tree branches hanging over the trail. We had to duck under anything we couldn't push aside with a hand or walking pole. The bright sunshine emerged from the gray clouds, offering a beautiful sight. However, it acted as a double agent, not only warming the walker but also transforming the ground beneath their feet. The snow became slush, which soon became mud, and doing tree-dodging squats while carrying a backpack AND trying not to lose a boot in the dirt became exhausting - fast.

Near a park, I located an outhouse—a generous description—where I could finally change my damp socks and use a toilet after many hours. *No lock on this door? Cool.* I changed my socks, though honestly, it felt fruitless as I already knew I had blisters. I taped the hot spots on my feet, and the dry socks felt better, and I regained some of my earlier optimism as I knew Pamplona wasn't far.

A full day of continuously sidestepping trees while wearing heavy, soaked, mud-encased boots left my legs crying in pain. Deciding to distract myself with musings of what it would be like once I reached Pamplona, I thought of a hot shower and warm, clean clothes. I imagined myself feeling revived and ready to explore the city. A restaurant filled with pilgrims enjoying a soothing meal. Boots that were dry and feet that didn't hurt.

A man with a box of fruit calling interrupted my thoughts and waved to me and a few other pilgrims nearby. He offered us oranges, apples and bananas for a few cents, and after the trek we had all just had, we were ready to pay up.

I bought an apple and munched on it as I went back to my daydreaming. After a few minutes, I found myself walking in step with another pilgrim, an American man about the same age as me. Our conversation began with the Camino, travels, family, and more. We got to talking about work and found that we had been in similar fields of home improvement and customer service. We had both endured a difficult period because of the pandemic. My habitual complaints resurfaced before I could even stop myself.

My companion shared many of the same complaints, and while "misery loves company", this was the noise I had wanted to quiet. Forgetting that I was equally capable of creating it. This pilgrim was a kind, upbeat guy, but the conversation left me depleted. I don't know if he felt the same; sometimes, cynical conversations can be hard to break out of. All I know is that the happy thoughts that had carried me along the soggy trail no longer felt strong enough to let Pamplona excite me.

Going out for a meal held no appeal for me. The timing was not right for the famous running of the bulls, and my level of appreciation for Ernest Hemingway was not so great that I felt compelled to make a pilgrimage to the locations where he spent his time. Instead, I opted for chips from the municipal albergue's vending machine and a cup of tea. I got my hot shower and started a load of laundry that I shared with my new friend. My walking buddy wanted to explore the town, so I volunteered to handle the laundry while he went out. When we'd first arrived earlier, the crowds had filled the streets, and restaurants were already getting ready for the evening rush of pilgrims.

I sat in my bunk and watched pilgrims come in and go right back out to have fun after walking all day. *How did they have any energy left? The book at the end of my bed might as well be miles away.* Dinner invitations came, and all of them got turned down. Socializing didn't appeal to me. Neither did talking; the afternoon had provided more than enough of that, and it wasn't a feeling worth repeating.

Reaching back to earlier in the day, before my sour mood kicked in, I tried to remember the night before— coffee and chocolates with new friends. That evening had provided reserves of joy I wanted to tap into, something to lift me off my bunk. Instead, the snores of my bunkmates lulled me into a grumpy slumber.

People had asked me several times throughout the day why I was doing the Camino, and I think my answer changed each time. I was walking to find God, to learn about myself, to change my lifestyle, to travel in a new way, and to test my boundaries. *Why was I here?*

Do you have a song that you sing to yourself when you're feeling motivated or trying to feel motivated? I guess mine is "Can't Get Next to You" by The Temptations. I found this out as I approached some intimidating inclines leaving Pamplona. Still a little sore from the day before but much more guarded against heavy intrusive thoughts, I was leaning on God and apparently Motown to guide me up Alto del Perdón.

Just as I hit the edge of town, I found my Lithuanian friend, Emilija, and we instantly gave each other a big hug before heading for the hills together. Even though we had met just three days before, it felt like reuniting with an old, close friend. Walking and talking with her proved to be the healing balm for the previous day's heaviness.

I have always been told that I walk a little too fast, but that was only from people who had never met Emilija. That girl can move.

I did my best to keep up with her and tried not to think about the soreness in my legs. The last of the surrounding snow was melting, and we were thrilled to put on our sunglasses! We hummed and zig-zagged our way up to the famous sculpture that sits atop Alto del Perdón. Monumento al Peregrino is a dramatic metal sculpture that depicts pilgrims en route to Santiago. They look as though they are fighting the wind, just as we were on top of this sacred peak.

The climb on the way down from the monument was brutal. It was steep, and loose stones covered the trail. A wrong step could easily lead to an injured ankle, so I tried to be careful whilst also not losing sight of Emilija. *Don't fall. Don't fall. Don't fall.* After a while, walking downhill on loose ground made my legs feel like jelly, and I was eager to get to more even ground.

It didn't help that I really needed to go to the bathroom. Emilija started jokingly pointing out shrubs and rocks that might provide cover for me. I am not opposed to peeing outside; I just needed a bathroom for that...week. We walked through a small town that didn't have any public restrooms, and I started taking a closer look at the shrubs. Thankfully, the next town, Obanos, wasn't too far, and I was saved.

Despite the many hills and small blisters from the previous day, I was feeling good. The snow and mud had nearly disappeared, and thanks to the bright sunshine, the temperature was warm enough to walk without multiple layers. Then, I did something new—I stopped for coffee along the trail itself. Up to this point, I'd only eaten and had coffee in the towns where I stayed for the night, always waiting until I reached my destination. But today felt different. When I ducked into a small cafe, familiar faces greeted me, and I realized I was among friends. Better yet, I was added to a WhatsApp group that included many of the people I'd met over the past three days. My Camino family was growing!

Our stopping point for that day was Puente la Reina. A beautiful town that I wanted to explore, but my stomach just wanted food. There was a cafe attached to the albergue, and though the full dinner menu didn't start until later, I could order a club sandwich. I knew I was gambling with my dietary restrictions, but I needed more than granola bars, and that sandwich tasted amazing. By the grace of God, I didn't feel sick.

The next morning, my muscles were really feeling it. I woke up with stiff legs and cranky knees. But it was another beautiful, sunny day, and I prayed it would put a spring in my step. Leaving Puente la Reina, the stunning scenery helped distract me from my aching bones. The fields surrounding the trail were lush and green, and some spring blooms were starting to show. The blizzard only two days prior seemed like a distant memory. Emilija and I walked together only a short distance on that day. The strain I felt made it seem like I was keeping a good pace, but she out-stepped me pretty quickly. Just after passing through the hilly town of Cirauqui, you come upon a Roman road. This was another instance where the historical heft of a place was overshadowed by my desire to just sit down. I was starting to feel downhearted when a couple of kind, older American pilgrims invited me to join them for lunch in Lorca.

My energy ebbed and flowed with the rolling hills surrounding me. I would have moments of such joy and laughter, and then pray with gritted teeth for my blisters to just disintegrate. My lunch companions had sped on ahead of me shortly after our meal. I could see that my body would not run on sunshine and friendly interactions for much longer.

This was what a pilgrimage was supposed to be, right? Pushing yourself to the absolute limit, hoping to touch the divine? I watched as the feet that were walking in time with mine moving ahead and my feet slowing down. *Everyone's passing me.* I always thought of myself as a relatively noncompetitive person; but I consistently checked the strides and breaks of other pilgrims against my own.

My hectic schedule, which led me to want a pilgrimage, came about for many reasons, but I can now see that comparison was a leading factor. The career I wanted, I didn't have. The talent I wanted, I didn't have. The physique I wanted, I didn't have. Now here, on the pilgrimage that promised provision, the endurance I wanted, I didn't have. I asked God for strength time and again, yet my body continued to beg for rest. *Why am I here?*

4

# Chapel Hours

I don't think we really know our habits until we try to break them. That's what led me to the Camino to begin with. I had patterns so deeply ingrained I couldn't see them anymore, let alone question them—a rhythm that desperately needed to be interrupted. Chief among them: a pathological inability to say no to people.

When the small church I attended asked if I'd be interested in joining their worship team, I said yes before I'd even thought it through. Why wouldn't I? I loved playing guitar and wanted to be of use. It felt good to be needed, to have something to contribute. And they wanted help.

There were three of us who shared the role of worship leader. We would rotate weeks of selecting songs and singing lead, but still all played some kind of guitar or percussion on our off weeks, rarely ever taking a week off. It started as something I genuinely enjoyed— a way to serve, to be part of something meaningful. Sunday mornings had their own rhythm: the smell of coffee in the church lobby, the sound check banter, the way certain songs could shift the energy in a room. I loved that. For a while, anyway.

But somewhere along the way, my love shifted to obligation. The songs became a checklist. The joy became a job. My doubts also overshadowed my desires; I doubted I could step back without letting everyone down, doubted that rest was allowed, and doubted that saying no was an option. I had served as a Sunday school teacher and youth director along with my friend Jess for a few years as well, and leaving those posts resulted in countless sleepless nights. *What if the kids feel abandoned? What if the program falls apart without us? What if we're being selfish?*

It turns out that saying yes to everything doesn't make you indispensable. It just makes you exhausted.

And then 2020 arrived, as if life decided I hadn't learned that lesson well enough yet.

In March of that year, the roads were completely empty, and I regularly glanced at the letter sitting on my passenger seat. *What is happening?* When I'd taken this job the year before, I had no idea that it would eventually require a letter from the government designating my work as essential. I worked at a large home improvement store. I imagined myself getting pulled over and having to explain, "It's okay for me to be out and about, officer—I sell paint!" It never came to that, of course. I never actually heard of anyone needing to show their "essential worker" letter, and after a few weeks, it didn't seem to matter anymore. The pandemic would surely be over by June. That was the expectation, anyway.

June came and went.

I remember customers coming in, glancing nervously around at us in our masks and face shields, wondering what the next mandate would bring—as if we, retail workers, would somehow have the inside scoop. (Spoiler: we didn't.) Each week brought a new set of changes implemented in the hopes of slowing down the spread of the virus, and each week brought out a new level of discontent from people unaccustomed to restrictions and waiting. The tension was palpable. Everyone was scared, frustrated, and angry at something they couldn't control, and we became convenient targets.

Wait times doubled, even tripled, for products as vendors cut back on labor. We were short-staffed, too. At one point, big box stores had to close certain departments considered cosmetic rather than essential—garden centers, paint departments. Those were a fun couple of weeks. My job transformed overnight from slinging paint cans to hauling lumber, appliances, and flooring, processing endless online orders, counting customers at the door, and cleaning. So much cleaning. I became intimately familiar with the smell of disinfectant and the weight of exhaustion that settles in your bones when you're running on adrenaline and fear.

But here's the thing about my inability to say no: it didn't stop at the church. It didn't stop at the store either.

Shortly before this chaos began, at the start of 2020, I'd launched my side business doing painting and upholstery work. Apparently, a full-time job and regular church commitments weren't quite enough to fill my schedule. I was worried that when the pandemic hit I wouldn't be able to continue, but surprisingly, I got a lot of gigs. At first, it was my quiet time—I could find zen painting a room or recovering a chair, losing myself in the work. For a couple of months, I did a series of small decor pieces inspired by children's books and enjoyed crafting for kids. There was something therapeutic about creating beauty in such an ugly time, about making something with my hands that had nothing to do with corporate policy or Sunday set lists.

But the more time people spent cooped up in their homes, the more desperately they wanted to change them. It became exponentially busier at the store, and I was fielding more and more calls for painting projects. The zen didn't last long. The side business that was supposed to be my creative outlet became just another obligation, another place where I couldn't say no, another source of pressure.

It became harder and harder to drag myself out of bed each morning, knowing full well I was going to get screamed at by a stranger for something completely outside my control—supply chain issues, product shortages, policies I didn't create. The anger people carried into that store was heavy and indiscriminate. We were just there, visible and available, easy recipients of their pandemic rage.

Add to that, I began losing sleep over my design business, plagued by anxiety that I'd start getting screamed at by clients too—for potentially messing up a wall or ruining a piece of furniture. Every request felt like a test I had to pass. I started feeling like I wasn't allowed to have time to rest, convinced that any downtime would make my clients think I wasn't giving them my best effort. I had genuinely kind and caring clients, but these intrusive thoughts piled up regardless, building and building until I wanted nothing more than to stop thinking altogether.

A brain vacation. That's what I wanted.

I was helping everyone else make their homes more beautiful while my own mental space was becoming uninhabitable.

I will say that despite everything those heavy pandemic years took from us—and they took so much— I became far closer to my family. The precautions we had to take and the physical space we had to maintain only heightened our awareness of how desperately we needed connection. When you can't casually drop by someone's house or give them a hug, you realize how much those small moments matter.

I started video chatting with my sisters regularly. We'd meet for walks in the park, gather in my parents' garage with the door open for ventilation, and find increasingly creative ways to stay in each other's lives. We learned to be intentional about it in ways we'd never had to be before. My family became my lifeline—not because we'd been distant, but because we'd taken proximity for granted. The pandemic stripped away that assumption and forced us to fight for closeness.

Those connections kept me afloat. They were the bright spots in an otherwise relentless grind.

But by the time restrictions began lifting and life started returning to some version of normal, I realized I'd been running on fumes for far too long. I experienced burnout in a way I didn't quite know how to name yet. The world was opening back up, but I felt like I was still trapped—not by lockdowns this time, but by the pace I'd maintained just to survive those years. Everyone was talking about getting "back to normal," but I couldn't remember what normal even felt like anymore.

The worship leading continued. The retail shifts continued. The side business continued. Everything continued except me—I was stuck, going through the motions of a life that no longer fit. I'd built a cage out of obligations and responsibilities, and I'd done it all to myself by never learning how to say that simple, necessary word: no.

I needed something to break the cycle. The heaviness of the pandemic, the political sphere, and the general attitude of customers were wearing on me, and I was becoming indifferent to it all. It's probably my biggest fear — feeling nothing. The anger I could handle—anger at least meant I still cared. But this creeping apathy? This sense that nothing really mattered anymore? That terrified me.

And then, because life apparently has a cruel sense of humor, I found out I was gluten, dairy, and egg intolerant.

One more thing I didn't need.

I'd been dealing with chronic stomach issues for a couple of years, dismissing them as stress-related. Which, to be fair, they probably were—at least partially. But after yet another round of doctors' appointments and elimination diets, the verdict came back: my body had rejected approximately eighty percent of the food I'd been eating my entire life. No more pizza. No more ice cream. No more grabbing something quick and easy when I was too exhausted to cook, because "quick and easy" usually meant gluten, dairy, or eggs—often all three.

It felt like a betrayal. My own body, the one thing I thought I could count on to just keep functioning if I pushed it hard enough, had apparently filed a formal complaint. And I had to listen.

Learning to navigate food intolerance while working with a hectic schedule meant meal planning became another item on my endless to-do list. Another thing to manage. Another source of anxiety when I'd go to someone's house for dinner and have to explain, apologize, and bring my own food. Another way I felt like I was being difficult, asking for too much, taking up too much space.

And yet, in those moments when the numbness was loudest, I knew I wasn't entirely alone.

I didn't like what I was doing for work, and I was trusting God with the rest, even when 'the rest' was a fog I couldn't see through. I had gone to school for writing but gave up on that dream a few years and a hundred rejections after graduating. The creative work I was doing through my side business should have been fulfilling, but the mixture of pressure and asking a reasonable price for my work was more stressful than I anticipated.

My journal entries from that time were filled with complaints and rants about the state of my life and the world at large, but over time, they turned into prayers. My moments with Jesus were the times I could feel the numbness subside, even just a little. I became more and more desperate for those moments as my schedule continued to fill up and my energy continued to dwindle. Those quiet spaces with God became the only thing keeping me tethered to myself.

My "chapel hours," as I called them, were my times where I would sit on the floor of my room and pull out my Bible and journal or guitar and wait on Jesus. Wait for a better job, wait to move into my own place, wait for a relationship, wait for things I couldn't even name, but whatever they were, I didn't have them yet.

The pandemic made me wait to travel—one of my favorite things in the world. While I waited to see the world again, I tried to see it through books. I found a book by Christian George called *Sacred Travels*, a collection of spiritual journeys that spoke to something deep inside me. Every chapter felt like a chapel hour to me, like I was being let in on a secret about what it meant to seek God not just in church pews or quiet rooms, but out in the wide world He'd made.

My mind had been full of anxiety over my jobs, finances, living situation, and then suddenly, a little room was made for a daydream about going on a pilgrimage. *Where would I go? When could I go? Could I actually do something like that?*

I dug through my pile of travel books and magazines and found all the pages I had bookmarked through the years—dog-eared corners and sticky notes marking places I'd told myself I'd visit "someday." And then I saw it.

El Camino de Santiago. The Way of Saint James.

I'd first read about the Camino years earlier, captivated by the idea of walking hundreds of miles through Spain, following the ancient route pilgrims had walked for over a thousand years. I'd tucked it away in my mental file of beautiful impossibilities—things that sounded wonderful but were unattainable, or at least unattainable until retirement.

But sitting there on my bedroom floor, surrounded by my travel magazines and my prayers and my desperate need for something to change, the Camino didn't feel impossible anymore. It felt necessary.

Burnout is a strange feeling. Wanting nothing more than to crawl out of what drives you to the brink, yet feeling obligated to stay in the car. I often thought that if I were to leave the things that caused me stress, I would be trading them in for another vehicle that was just as chaotic as the first.

So, I chose to walk.

*5*

# Attic Day

Have you ever cried over a *pain au chocolat*? Because I have! In public! It was on my first rest day, and I was saying goodbye to people I had known for less than a week. My friends were all continuing on, and I was staying another day in Estella. After a lengthy internal debate, I decided I needed a break. Before leaving on the Camino, I fantasized about the idea of becoming someone who would take their time, have moments of pause and reflection, and enjoy solitude. Only now I didn't want to pause. I wanted to continue with my new friends; it was my body telling me to stop.

I didn't expect to make connections so quickly and to have to part with them just as quickly. We all had coffee that morning, and after the hugs, I was left alone at a table, so I ordered a pastry and more coffee. I was fully intent on making this day worth the sadness I felt. With my guidebook open and phone ready, I tried to read about Estella for an hour. I really just wanted to go back to the albergue I shared with my friends.

Closing my eyes, I imagined myself sitting in the back garden the previous night and not sitting all alone in a crowded cafe.

There was something about that garden that made me want to ingrain it in my memory. Everything about it was inviting. Small potted plants embellished the vibrant terracotta orange paint on the walls surrounding the small patch of green. Pilgrims scattered themselves on benches, grass, picnic tables, or lone plastic chairs. Some were on their phones; some were snacking or chatting with friends. And then there were some who sat basking in the sun. I had sipped my tea and scribbled in my journal, occasionally eating a chocolate cookie.

I love the patina of pilgrim dwellings. Whether it be a newer albergue or an ancient monastery, the continuous passing of people has left an indelible mark. Nothing is too precious or designed "just so" that might make the traveler hesitant to drop their gear. Having Covid precautions in place, hostels took more care for cleanliness and sanitation, but the patina remains.

Now back in the cafe, I opened my eyes and gave up on my reading. I slowly gathered my things and walked into the colorful town. I made my way to my new albergue and was able to check in early and leave my backpack while I explored Estella. Most albergues only allow you to stay one night as they need to clean the entire place to get ready for a new set of pilgrims coming in each day.

I found an open grocery store that had a gluten-free section, and I almost cried for the second time that day. Into my basket went some bread and jamón to make sandwiches, as well as some granola bars, clementines and a couple of apples. The day before, I had stopped at a small bodega and was looking for a snack. After asking the man at the counter if he had anything gluten-free, he walked over to a shelf and grabbed a package of chocolate sandwich cookies. Happily handing them to me, he said, "These are not gluten-free, but they are really good." So I bought them.

I wrote some goals in my journal for this day of rest. My plan included reading my Bible, spending time in prayer, and reviewing my first few days as a pilgrim. None of that happened. I sat in the garden of my new albergue with a cup of tea and enjoyed the sunshine for a couple of hours before taking a shower. Whatever thoughts filled my mind that afternoon have vanished now, and looking back at my journal, I see all I had written was that I felt rested. Things can only go up from here, right?

My dad came up with the phrase "attic day" to describe the days when something happens that causes every curse word you've ever heard to fly out of your mouth and paint the room blue. This name came from the day he accidentally put his foot through the attic floor (and subsequently his bedroom ceiling). I was outside on my "attic day", so I didn't paint any rooms blue, but a couple of squirrels had to cover their ears.

The day I left Estella started out good, great even. I woke up feeling rested and hopeful. As you leave town, you come across the Bodegas Irache Wine Fountain. A beautifully ornate fountain that brings forth wine pressed by monks. I saw a few familiar faces that I had met in Roncesvalles, and we all took turns getting pictures and drinking from the famous fountain. Some pilgrims fill a water bottle, and some, like me, fill their scallop shells and try not to spill any wine down their chin as they sip. After wiping away what missed my mouth, I said, "Buen Camino" to my friends and continued on. It was another sunny day so I planned to have a trail-side picnic before reaching Los Arcos, my stopping point for the day.

Although I had slept well and rested my feet, I was still incredibly sore. The worst pain was in my knees. I had read about hiker's knee, muscle and joint pain caused by frequent descents. I had done enough of those over the past few days to accept that as my diagnosis. The remedy was the usual rest and elevation, which I had done the day before and intended to do that evening.

I really wanted to enjoy hiking through the olive groves and tried to slow down to appreciate stepping on an ancient Roman road. The sunshine was a buffer to my discouragement of walking with sore legs. I stopped for my trail-side picnic and ate one of my gluten-free jamón sandwiches I had made the night before and a couple of clementines. After about fifteen minutes of enjoying my food and a brief break, I stood up and got ready to descend yet another hill.

I had barely taken two steps down this hill when I felt my left knee lock. Though the popping noise didn't echo through the valley, it rang in my ears. I felt a shock of pain climb from my knee up to my teeth! My eyes welled with tears, and I started shaking my leg, trying to get my knee to bend. (And this is when the swearing started.) I was being passed by a few groups of pilgrims who looked on with some concern but ultimately kept walking as they probably didn't know what to do with a woman angrily shaking her leg.

My knee bent after what felt like ages of painful paralysis. I tentatively stepped forward with my left foot and put some pressure on it. *Please don't lock, please don't lock.* It didn't. But it hurt like a mother. I shuffled slowly down the hill, clenching my teeth with each step. Having made it to more even ground, I stopped and found a large rock to sit on. I rubbed my knee as I lowered myself onto the boulder, checking to see if anything felt loose. I had bought a knee brace to help with the soreness I was already experiencing and pulled that over my throbbing leg.

According to my guidebook, Los Arcos was about four kilometers away. Wiping my tears, I braced myself for the slowest hike of my life. I stood up a little too quickly and felt my knee lock again. *No, no, no!* I tried to be gentler in my leg shaking as more pilgrims were passing me and staring. My knee loosened, and I very slowly started making my way towards Los Arcos.

My tears of pain turned into tears of anger. *How could I be so stupid to think I was in shape? Should I even be walking on this leg? What if I did some permanent damage? Do I have to quit?* I stopped once or twice more before I saw the edge of town. In my mind, I pictured a glistening city with a nurse and a wheelchair waiting at the gate for me. I'd float over to the chair and get wheeled off to a handsome doctor who would tell me it's an easy fix and I'd be better by morning.

A chicken.

That's who greeted me on my way into Los Arcos. It stood right in the middle of the path as if it knew about my daydream and just wanted to taunt me. I made a face at it as I passed and waddled my way through town until I found an albergue. By the time I arrived, only top bunks were available, and I learned the kitchen was up two flights of stairs. *Looks like jamón and clementines for a second time today.*

I threw my things onto my bunk and took a shower, hoping that the warm water might ease some of the knee pain. There were a couple of picnic tables in the common area and more outdoors on the patios. I propped my leg up on a bench seat and pulled out my phone. I wanted to talk to my family, but felt that I was still on the verge of tears. The pain had subsided a bit, but I was still angry. I decided to go down the internet rabbit hole of possible injuries and remedies.

My knee may have suffered a torn meniscus, but I wouldn't know for sure until I saw a doctor. I weighed my options and looked at the risks of walking with a bad knee. After several minutes of getting mixed answers from different sites, I put my phone down and sighed. In the corner of my eye, I saw a hand waving. An elderly woman sat on the other side of the room, knitting needles and yarn resting in her lap. She waved to me, and I waved back.

Without saying a word, she pointed to her feet, and I watched as she shifted them from side to side. She then pointed to my feet, gesturing for me to do the side steps as well. I slowly placed my feet on the floor, and from both our seats on either side of the room, this sweet lady and I did some simple foot exercises. I had almost forgotten how broken I felt in those few minutes, but when I stood up to get some water, I was quickly reminded by my stupid, stupid knee.

*I don't want to quit! I just got here!* I could feel my frustration rising again when I overheard someone asking one of the albergue hosts about a bus route. Other pilgrims had already waited at bus stops, but I was convinced I would never join them. Out came my phone to look up Camino bus routes, and I felt as though my journey might not be over. Taking the bus wasn't something I wanted to do, but I also didn't want to sit on my butt all day and watch people pass. I had done that in Estella. (Funny how easy rest gets relabeled as laziness when you're pissed off, isn't it?)

Now that I had a plan in mind, I mustered up the courage to call my family and check in with them, as I had done every day so far. I called my older sister, Jill, first. After relaying the events of the day to her, she knew what would help me feel better. After handing the phone over to her two-year-old daughter, I got to spend ten blissful minutes talking about *Bluey* and strawberries with one of my very favorite people. I called my parents next and told them about my knee and how I was hoping to take the bus the next day. They were just glad that I was safe and encouraged me to pray about it and listen to my body. I hung up, still not feeling totally peaceful but slightly better about the coming day.

My mom and dad had written me letters I was to open on the eighth day of my walk. It was day seven, and I wanted all the encouragement that I could get, so I opened the letters a day early. My parents had written wonderful notes of encouragement and hope, but the words came with a sting. They had timed it out so that I would open their letters after I had walked 100 miles. They congratulated me on the milestone that I had yet to make and at that moment wasn't sure I was going to.

*6*

# The Goose Game

Sleep did not come easily, if at all, that night. On top of the knee injury, I was sharing a room with pilgrims who seemed to be part of a snoring symphony orchestra. Earplugs were not enough to block the noise as just when one snorer would *diminuendo*, another would *crescendo*. The pilgrim in the bed beneath mine must have been the tuba in this arrangement as his breathing was *FORTISSIMO*. His baritone snores reverberated through the bunk frame; shaking me awake with each thunderous inhale.

I don't remember looking in a mirror the following morning, which is probably for the best. No need for an image of a disheveled gargoyle to be embedded in my memory.

I moved so slowly I could count my individual steps without looking at the pedometer on my watch as I shuffled to the bus stop. *One year. I have been thinking, planning, and praying about this pilgrimage for one year.* I watched the other pilgrims turn toward the yellow arrows. *This is pathetic. One week in, and I'm moving at a snail's pace. From walking down a flipping hill! Ugh.*

My knee was throbbing, and each step felt like my joints were engaged in a jousting tournament. Pilgrims usually gave a courteous "Buen Camino" in passing, but on this day, the combination of my limp and the storm cloud I wore like a hat must have been a deterrent.

Arriving at the bus stop, I looked around at the other pilgrims waiting to board the bus, and their condition humbled me. While I had shown up with a noticeable awkward gait, there were some with bandages around their ankles and braces on their legs. Some had to forgo shoes as they were suffering from brutal blisters. There were a few leaning on friends as standing was too much. I overheard an English woman encourage another limping pilgrim, "Don't let anyone put you down for this! It's called the *Way* of St. James, not the *walk* of St. James, and the bus is on the way." *God bless her.*

The bus arrived, and we all slowly boarded. I don't remember whether the bus was crowded or spacious, but I saw a young woman from my albergue and asked if I could sit with her. This bus ride probably could have been used to prop my leg up and mentally mope about my injury, but for some reason, I decided to sit with a stranger.

She smiled and welcomed me to the empty seat. One thing that I love about traveling is that when you meet new people, you never just get their name. Like a medieval herald, you get their homeland as well: Hugh of England, Therese of France, Manuel of Brazil! Though I live in the U.S., I am Canadian, and many years of travel have taught me that when introducing myself abroad, go with Canada. So I, Amy of Canada, found myself sitting next to Kathrine of Denmark.

As we spoke, I looked out the window, watching the kilometers tick by that I wouldn't be walking. The distance to Logroño wasn't impossible, maybe twenty-eight kilometers, but after what my knee had been through the day before, it felt insurmountable. *Am I giving up too easily?* Part of me wrestled with guilt, like I was cheating the Camino somehow. But the other part knew that pushing through would only make things worse. Kathrine told me about the hotel she was staying in for the night and suggested I stay at the same place. I had been sleeping in albergues only so far, sharing rooms with strangers and their snores, and the thought of a hotel room felt both indulgent and necessary. *A bed to myself. A door that locks. Quiet.* I wasn't sure if I deserved it, but Kathrine assured me I did. The bus hummed along the route I would have walked, and I tried to let go of the guilt, focusing instead on the fact that taking this break meant I could keep going. That had to count for something.

We arrived in Logroño too early to check into the hotel, so we went in search of coffee. Along the way, we stumbled upon a park filled with strange exercise structures that looked too bizarre to ignore. At parks back home, only kids get equipment to play on, adults get a bench or a sidewalk. Since Kathrine and I were both nursing injuries, we stuck to the equipment that required little climbing or coordination. There were oddly shaped stationary bikes, pull-up bars for the optimistic, metal wheels you could spin with your arms—either for exercise or to pretend you were steering a very slow ship—and something that had handlebars jutting out in every conceivable direction, like a mechanical octopus frozen mid-reach. Much like at the gym back home, I had no clue how to use half of it, and I'm fairly certain we didn't use the other half correctly either. But we gave it a whirl anyway.

We enjoyed a coffee together before we found our way to La Iglesia de Santiago Real. As we slowly walked through the cathedral, I realized this was the first time I was actively reading the surrounding plaques. Nearly every town I had walked through had plaques describing a building or structure of significance, and I had walked right on by. Trying to keep up the pace instead of taking in my surroundings was an unfortunate trade. *What other moments have I unknowingly traded?* I'm not sure how long we spent inside the church, but it was long enough for me to remember the feeling of the smooth wooden pews and the shade of green paint behind the figure of the Madonna and Child. The sun was blinding as I stepped out of the dimly lit sanctuary, and my eyes instinctively darted to the ground where they latched onto a goose.

In the Plaza de Santiago, laid in stone, is the Goose Game. A popular European board game that has become associated with the Camino. The dice game, made up of white images of geese, saints and towns along the Camino, was an inviting activity for two women who honestly had nothing else to do. This was one of the rare times I didn't consult my guidebook before trying something, but Katherine and I rolled some dice (through an app) and moved from square to square. We had no idea what we were doing, but we had a good time. We both won. I think. That's when I realized I had a new friend in Kathrine. We made time to play.

She and I wandered to about three different cafes that day, watching the Spanish rhythm of life unfold around us. The sun warmed our faces while we nursed our coffees, in no particular hurry to be anywhere else. And the orange juice—*the orange juice*—was mind-blowingly good. Fresh-squeezed and almost impossibly sweet, it tasted like liquid sunshine in a glass. I'd order another just to make the moment last a little longer, devoted entirely to the simple pleasure of sunshine, citrus, and giving my battered knee a break.

How might this day have been different had I not taken the bus? I imagine that I would have just arrived in Logroño and immediately gone to an albergue and moped the rest of the day. I would have eaten a granola bar, drunk a vending machine coffee, and sat in my bunk. Another day lost.

It was early afternoon when we arrived at the hotel. We got our pilgrim passports stamped and headed up to our rooms, which were right next door to each other. This hotel stay was only sixty euros and after spending a week in ten euro a night hostels, this place felt like the height of luxury. I unpacked my bag and let it air out, then took advantage of the bathtub I didn't have to share with forty-five other people.

After a lovely bath, I searched for nearby takeaway places and discovered a paella shop around the corner. I texted Kathrine to join me. We grabbed our dinners, said "see you tomorrow," and headed back to our rooms for the night. I stacked some pillows, propped up my leg, and dove into my paella and VERY garlicky broccoli. I pulled out my maps and studied the next day's stage. The Camino has suggested stages for each day, and I'd been following them so far. I decided to shorten my days for a while to rest my knee, planning to make up the distance later on.

There is another kind of rest that comes with having your own space. There is no one around to compare yourself to. I would normally look around, seeing who still has energy to go out and explore, who's sleeping, stretching, socializing. There might be a pilgrim cooking a well-rounded meal or one with a protein bar. I would sometimes sit in my bunk and think, *Okay, what am I supposed to be doing?* But in looking around my empty hotel room, I can clearly see what would have been muffled by comparing myself to others — *rest.*

The "magic" of the Camino—Kathrine and I couldn't stop talking about it. Even though I'd dismissed this as a cheat day, the magic showed up anyway. Meeting her was exactly what I needed. I woke up the next morning refreshed and motivated, knee pain notwithstanding.

Before Kathrine left, I headed out, trusting we'd reconnect on the trail.

As you exit Logroño, you pass by some underwhelming urban and industrial businesses before being blessed with walking through Parque Grajera. A charming park, home to small ponds, manicured hedges, sweet wooded areas, and well-maintained paths. It was here that I ran into my old buddy, Dan. He was having the time of his life watching the wildlife scamper across the trail, and it made him look like a little kid at the zoo. We walked and chatted together about life, faith, and ducklings. The little red squirrels in this park were not shy, so when I held out a piece of my granola bar, a couple of them climbed right onto my hand to take some.

There was a man, who I assume worked at the park, with pockets full of seeds and nuts, ready to share. He didn't speak to Dan and me; he just took our hands and beckoned his woodland friends to come and sit in our hands and wait for a treat. *This is absurd. I love it.* I felt like I was on those nature shows with Steve Irwin gushing over a lizard. But I was with Dan and some mystery man, making friends with squirrels. I have no idea how much time I spent in that park. I remember looking for nests, pointing out turtles, trying to whistle with grass between my thumbs, and wishing I could freeze time.

Speaking of time, I don't think I had let the age of this pilgrimage really sink in until I reached Navarrete. Just before entering the town, you pass the ruins of the Hospital de San Juan de Acre, a hospital founded in the 12th century for pilgrims en route to Santiago de Compostela. I stood in front of the plaque and tried to picture pilgrims in the Middle Ages wearily coming to the hospital after a long day of walking in leather shoes and a cloth bag over their shoulder.

Moving through town, I arrived at Iglesia Nuestra Señora de la Asunción. This church was built in the 1500s, and you can just walk in. No velvet ropes, no ticket booth, no guard telling you to step back. History isn't something you observe from a distance here; it's the floor beneath your feet, the air you breathe as you stand where people have stood for five hundred years.

I sat at a cafe outside the cathedral and watched the light shift across its facade. My mind wandered through the centuries—merchants and pilgrims, wars and quiet Sundays, the countless ordinary moments that had unfolded in this same square. The church had witnessed it all, and now it was witnessing me, a stranger with a coffee, trying to fathom the weight of all that time. Kathrine pulled up a chair next to me, interrupting my thoughts.

She and I discovered we were part of the same Camino family and knew most of the same people, we had just been playing an accidental game of tag up to this point. We walked to our next albergue together, run by an elderly man known to us as "Abuelo."

When Kathrine's walking poles went missing, Abuelo swooped in like a fairy godfather and made sure she left with a shiny new pair. We woke to cloudy skies after a solid night of sleep, hoping the sun would break through as the day progressed. It was strange to think that just a couple of days before; I thought my pilgrimage was over. My knee was still tender, but thanks to Kathrine and her easy company, this silly goose was waddling on.

7

# Heart of Gold

I passed 160 kilometers (100 miles) of walking that day. If I had been able to walk to Logroño, I would have hit it two days earlier. But even though it felt like an accomplishment, I was tired. Arriving in Nájera, I had a hard time finding an albergue that wasn't fully booked. The municipal albergue had a line of pilgrims waiting outside, and I joined them, hoping that I wouldn't have to walk another six kilometers to Azofra or, worse, another fifteen kilometers to Cirueña. Thankfully, it didn't come to that.

I found a lot of comfort in talking to my family each night and unpacking the day with them. My albergue didn't have Wi-Fi, so I couldn't do that. *And wasn't that the whole point? Unplugging and just being present?* I had wanted this. You go through waves of emotions on the trail. Each new day brought a new place and new people. I met a pilgrim from Belgium whose bunk was across from mine. He was a man of sweeping gestures and greeted me with a kiss on the hand and a teasing smirk. I liked him immediately.

The dormitory was packed, and the night played out in whispers, snores, grunts, and one couple's argument that desperately needed to be taken outside. The morning came, and my eyes moved around the room as weary people slowly stretched and got ready for another day on the road. I sighed before reaching for my gear. *Today is Palm Sunday.*

Leaving Nájera on Palm Sunday morning, I thought about what worship was supposed to look like. Palm branches and processional hymns would fill the churches, but I preferred something quieter—something more intimate. I had spent so much of my life singing in sanctuaries, but here, walking through the vineyards of La Rioja, I could worship by simply being present in creation. The rolling hills stretched out before me, row after row of gnarled vines waiting for spring, and I walked in silence, letting the landscape speak for itself. *This is worship too.*

It was another shorter day, but it was good. I didn't listen to any music, just walked in awe of the creation around me. After some time alone with my thoughts and with God, I met up with Kathrine and our young Australian friend, Leo, along with his dad, James. Leo was making friends easily and had gathered many Camino "brothers," "sisters," and "cousins." Being twice his age earned me the title of Camino "aunt", a role I was more than happy to claim.

Kathrine and I would tease and laugh with him, finding that silliness came easily when the three of us were together. I was still in pain and moving slowly, so my Camino "nephew" would bounce between walking ahead with his father and hanging back with the "limpin' ladies." It was fun walking with them for a while, even though I tended to walk faster when I was around others, which hurt my knee quite a bit. But we made it fifteen kilometers to our albergue in Cirueña.

We had already booked our albergue for the following day since it was Holy Week and the Camino was much busier than it had been. We'd been reserving in advance whenever we could, trying to stay ahead of the surge of pilgrims. I was concerned about the end of the week in Burgos; finding a place to stay in a larger city during Holy Week felt like a gamble. I didn't like the bed race. It added unnecessary stress to the Camino, turning what should have been a spiritual journey into a competitive scramble. *This isn't what I signed up for.*

My knee was a lot more red and swollen than I had thought. Looking at it in the afternoon light, I could see the inflammation creeping around my kneecap, angry and tender to the touch. I met a nice German woman named Lina, and we sat in the sun together, comparing our battle wounds. She also had a knee injury—hers wrapped in a compression sleeve that looked far more professional than my haphazard approach. We pulled up our pant legs to get some sun on them, hoping the warmth might do something, anything, to ease the ache. I was wondering if I was pushing a little too hard. My knee didn't feel much better despite the rest days I'd taken, and I didn't want to sit on my butt all the time. Caring for it properly mattered to me, and I was tempted to take the bus again, even if only to help with the logistics of finding a place to stay in Burgos.

On top of all that, I was also sporting a sun-imposed stripe across my forehead from my bandana—courtesy of no sunscreen. To prevent that from happening again, I had bought what I thought was a roll-on sunscreen at a small shop in town. Turns out, it was basically a glue stick for your face. I tried rubbing it on, and it just sat there in waxy streaks, refusing to blend. *Perfect. Just perfect.*

Icing my knee right before bed helped me ease into a comfortable position, but it didn't last. We had one late-arriving pilgrim who apparently believed that setting up his bed by headlamp wouldn't disturb anyone. Every slight turn of his head meant his searchlight found a new set of eyes to blind, and you never knew when it was going to be your turn. We all shifted and fidgeted, trying to avoid the sweeping beam, which meant I was twisting and turning with a knee that wanted nothing to do with either of those movements. *Dude, pleeeeeaaaaase just stop moving.* And of course, this guy was an early riser too.

Morning came, and it hurt. Everything hurt. My knee was red and swollen, and now my feet had joined the chorus of complaints. My roommates in Cirueña convinced me to send my backpack ahead to our albergue in Redecilla del Camino. There is a courier service pilgrims can use to ease their journey and send their gear to their next stop for only five euros. Five euros well spent. *Best decision I've made in days.* I walked in sandals to let my aching feet breathe, and luckily; it was a warm and sunny day, so the sandals and lack of weight on my back were ideal. My shoulders felt lighter, my stride a little less labored.

We arrived at our albergue in Redecilla del Camino and were met by our host, whom I'll refer to as Gregorio, after the patron saint of singers (you'll see why). He spoke very little English and was checking in a Spanish couple when Kathrine and I arrived. Along with a large table in the soft pink dining room was a piano, guitar, bookshelf, fireplace, and my backpack! He gestured to his guitar in the corner and invited us to occupy ourselves with it while we waited. I picked it up and plucked out a few notes while Gregorio showed the other pilgrims to their room.

After a while, he came back and smiled when he saw me holding the guitar. This man's smile took up his entire face, and it was radiant. Gregorio told us he would make us a delicious dinner, and we could go meet the other pilgrims staying there while we waited. Kathrine and I joined a small group of people hanging out on a playground near the albergue. There were seven of us sprawled on the ground with our feet up on the climbing net, sitting on swings, and riding a spring horse. Alba and Javier from Spain, Paul from Canada, Marcel from France, and Hannu from Finland. Kathrine and I were the youngest of this eclectic group by about twenty years, but it didn't matter. On that playground, we were all six-year-olds. Gregorio opened the kitchen window, and we could hear him sing as he prepared our meal.

It felt good to just stretch out, and we all took turns putting our feet up on the net and enjoyed spreading our arms and legs like starfish, regardless of how it looked. After spending a good amount of time outside, I went in and sat down at the table with Alba. She didn't speak any English but was adamant that we could communicate just fine.

My mediocre Spanish education reared its head when she asked me what living in Michigan was like, and I described the "Great Lakes State" as "mucho agua". I deferred to a translation app, and we continued to share our homes with each other. Alba was so patient with me when I fumbled my words and was kind enough to speak slowly for me to understand her better. She was from Ponferrada and loved her hometown. She told me we would pass through it on the Camino and encouraged me to spend time in this place she loved so much. I promised her I would.

Alba asked to see pictures of where I grew up and what I loved about where I live. Though I've lived in Michigan most of my life, it's not often that people ask me why I live there. Out came pictures of Grand Traverse Bay and Sleeping Bear Dunes. I showed her my favorite park to walk in Grand Rapids and told her how I can visit my family and friends in Canada as often as I like. Of course, I held up my hand and showed Alba where on "the mitten" I lived, and she laughed.

Dinner didn't start until 9 p.m., and we were all hungry. When Gregorio came out with the food, he carefully served each person, and then himself. He had made soup, pasta, bread, and apple pie all from scratch. I didn't have the heart to deny any of the beautiful meal and decided to endure whatever digestive consequences were to come from it. We ate, passed the wine, and talked throughout the meal. It was absolutely delicious food, and the company made it all the better. Marcel went out of the room after the food was cleared and returned with his guitar and a tablet. He said that he loved to sing with pilgrims and had music from all over the world on his tablet for us to choose from.

It was 10 p.m., and we were full from the meal. Seeing that Marcel was gearing up for a full sing-along, we were all a little leery. But then he started playing "Hotel California" and all of us started singing along. He played traditional Spanish, Danish, and Finnish songs. He played classic rock songs in English and a song or two in French. After a while, Marcel asked if anyone else played guitar, and I slowly raised my hand.

I have played the guitar since I was fifteen years old, but at that moment; I forgot everything I knew about music. I couldn't even remember worship songs I've played for half my life that are only four chords! My mind was blank, and I looked desperately at Marcel, and he suggested he play a Beatles song, and I was off the hook.

I wasn't as embarrassed as I might have been in any other setting. That wasn't the tone in this room. There was too much camaraderie for humiliation. From my time talking with Alba, to lounging with my new friends on the playground and then singing loudly in languages I didn't know, I felt kind of liberated from embarrassment.

In the movie *Eat, Pray, Love*, Liz Gilbert travels to Italy to rediscover her appetite for life. She makes some friends along the way who become like family. In my favorite scene, she is having Thanksgiving dinner with her Italian family, and the song "Heart of Gold" by Neil Young plays in the background. Here I was sitting around a Spanish table with my pilgrim family, and Gregorio picked up his harmonica and played, "Heart of Gold". It was such a surreal moment I couldn't help but tear up.

It was a fun, full night, and after the hour-long singalong, we were all more than ready for bed. Paul, Hannu, Kathrine and I were all in one room together, Alba and Javier in another, and Marcel in his RV. It had begun to rain, and there was a low rumble of thunder in the distance. I have always found thunderstorms soothing, so sleep was coming easily to me - until there was a loud banging noise on the door! Kathrine shot out of her bed, opened the door, and Alba ran into the room. She was speaking rapidly and waving her arms excitedly. Kathrine was trying to ask her, "What's wrong? Are you okay? Why are you pointing at the window?"

Alba rushed past her, opened the curtains, and pointed outside. *Was she just trying to tell us it's raining?* She stopped speaking for a moment; her face glued to the window. Then, a bright flash of lightning seemed to split the entire sky in half! More and more flashes danced across the distance, and Alba hopped, pointing and smiling at the light show that now served as the encore to our entertainment for the night.

*8*

# Sabbath

It took my knee a long time to settle into the rhythm of walking the next day. My head and my heart felt as though they were in a fog from the experience at Gregorio's. Kathrine and I were walking to Belorado to catch the bus to Burgos, a few days ahead of schedule, but we had heard from others in our Camino family that places were booking up for the busy Easter weekend. I didn't feel so guilty about taking the bus this time around, as we were just trying to make sure we would get there in time to have a place to stay and would beat the crowds. Semana Santa (Holy Week) is a huge deal in Spain, and many cities, including Burgos, have parades and floats, music and feasts for the entire week leading up to Easter.

I was excited to experience Easter traditions different from my own, but the truth was, I felt just as content celebrating in a smaller town, away from the crowds and large-scale festivities.

We ran into one of our roommates from Cirueña, an American pilgrim named Jennie, along the way and spent some time chatting about our plans in Burgos. After pausing the conversation so we could all have a snack and drink some water, Jennie looked at me with that direct, unflinching gaze of hers and asked, "So tell me, Amy, is it just your knee, or do you feel like all of you is completely f—-d up?"

I spat my water.

*Is that what it looks like?*

"I hope it's just my knee," I said, forcing a laugh that came out more nervous than casual. "But then again, I did just quit my jobs and buy a one-way ticket to Spain, so who knows?"

That was some heavy food for thought as I sat on the bus to Burgos, watching the Spanish countryside blur past the window. And then, a miracle.

I fell asleep.

Coffee was the first thing on my mind when we arrived in Burgos. The surprise bus ride nap had left me groggy. We found a cozy cafe near the Catedral de Santa María—the kind of place with worn wooden tables and the smell of espresso permanently embedded in the walls. I ordered chicken wings, fries, and a strong coffee, and I felt a small sense of normalcy return as I bit into the crispy, salty food. It was simple. It was delicious. It was exactly what I needed.

And best of all, I spotted a couple of friends I had said goodbye to in Estella, my early Camino family. We hugged tightly and exchanged brief stories of what we'd missed while apart, and it was as though I was laughing with friends I've had for much longer than just a couple of weeks.

After lunch, Kathrine and I made our way toward the cathedral, and the moment I stepped inside, I forgot how to breathe.

It was the most incredible cathedral I had ever seen! Beautiful didn't even begin to cover it—awe-inspiring, breathtaking, almost incomprehensible in its detail.

Everywhere I looked, there were sculptures of Jesus and the disciples. Statues and paintings of Mary occupied every alcove and altar. And the glass *(sigh), the glass.* It bathed the domed sanctuary in a kaleidoscope of color.

I felt true, authentic, unfiltered wonder. There were intricate, illuminated carvings of the Gospel stories embedded in the walls and golden altars that gleamed in the daylight that spilled through the ornate windows. It left you breathless. *How did human hands create this?* I wondered. *How many years? How many souls poured their devotion into these stones?* I get tingles down my spine even now, thinking about it.

It felt ostentatious in one moment—almost too much, too shiny, too grand—but deeply reverent in the next. There was a sculpture depicting the Ascension that made me tear up. Another captured a moment in the garden before the crucifixion, Jesus kneeling in anguish, and it was so moving I had to look away. There was even a Leonardo da Vinci painting! The painting's placement in one of the side chapels felt surreal, like stumbling upon a secret the world had forgotten.

As I stood there, surrounded by centuries of faith rendered in stone and glass, a question rose in my mind: *What does it take for us to remember God?*

Do we need monuments like this? Bright stained glass and shiny altars to remind us we care? Maybe we do. I'd often been judgmental of such grandeur, priding myself on loving simplicity and stripped-down faith. But there had been so many times on this trip when I'd wanted, tried, to focus on God, and it had been hard. Even the simplicity of pilgrim life, with its rhythms of walking and sleeping and eating, could be enough of a distraction. The physical pain, the exhaustion, the constant motion—it all pulled me away from the quiet space where God felt near.

Right after we left, Kathrine and I both took a deep breath, as if we'd been holding it the entire time we were inside. No words fit what we'd just experienced, so we said nothing. We walked quietly down the cathedral steps, past a few shops, until I saw one that was selling rosaries.

I'd been wanting to get one since I started the Camino; I don't know why. That day, I finally found the one. It was simple, small, with pink wooden beads and a small image of the Virgin Mary. A delicate crucifix hung at the end. There was no distinct reason for wanting one. I just did.

*Maybe this rosary will help me remember to rely on Him more*, I thought as I turned it over in my hands, feeling the smooth beads between my fingers. The problem was, I had no idea how to pray the rosary. *Who am I to limit myself to only the traditions I'm accustomed to?* I was walking an ancient path—maybe some ancient traditions held more revival, more life, than I'd ever expected.

Maybe I needed to stop being so afraid of what I didn't understand. Maybe that was part of the lesson, too.

The following morning began with very stiff and sore knees, but it was Kathrine to the rescue with ice and coffee! Starting our day slowly was exactly what our aching bones needed. We left our hotel to explore Burgos and were quickly distracted by a beautiful window display of pastries and cakes. A treat was in order—we each got two desserts. Kathrine and I walked through the stunning medieval side of Burgos and found a spot on a bridge bedecked with statues to sample our first treat.

I loved the beautiful trees and topiaries that lined the streets. I loved sipping my coffee and watching locals and pilgrims pass and lose themselves in the postcard of a city. You could hear the faint sound of music playing from inside the cafes and shops; it felt like a place stuck in time. It was blissful, and then, every so often, I would get flashes in my mind of the monks from *Monty Python and the Holy Grail* that chant and smack themselves with planks of wood - like an omen warning me of enjoying myself too much. This was a pilgrimage after all, not a vacation. Rest from the stresses of life—that's what I'd come to Spain wanting to find, yet somehow I mentally fought that rest at every turn, as if it were something I had to deny myself rather than receive. The feeling that I hadn't earned it yet kept nagging at me. I had blistered feet, sore joints, an injured knee, and a funky sunburn; was that enough?

Were there rules on this journey I was unknowingly breaking? Staying in a hotel, sitting down for coffee, choosing comfort over austerity—was I doing pilgrimage wrong?

I was definitely breaking dietary rules by consuming pastries and cakes at an alarming rate, but somehow that felt so much more justifiable in my head. (My stomach had different opinions, but I chose to ignore those.)

Kathrine and I spent the afternoon slowly exploring Burgos, sporting the universally recognized pilgrim uniform of socks with sandals while munching on chocolate-covered pastries. We admired shop windows and wandered down narrow cobblestone lanes that opened unexpectedly onto grand boulevards. Everything about our demeanor gave a relaxed impression, but beneath it, a familiar voice nagged: *If I'm strong enough to wander through town, shouldn't I be on the road?*

I'm glad I didn't let that intrusive thought win out in the end. Burgos is one of the most stunning towns I have ever been to, and I would have missed so much if I'd rushed through it.

This beautiful, aged city revealed itself in layers—contrasts tucked into every corner. The well-kept, sculpted foliage of the manicured streets was cleanly spaced between old statues with moss clinging to their weathered stone faces. New and ancient, existing side by side. Polished café windows reflected crumbling medieval walls. Tour buses idled near footpaths worn smooth by a thousand years of pilgrims' feet.

As I walked, my mind went to the practice of Sabbath—a full day of rest that God didn't just recommend but commanded. *Commanded.* Growing up, I'd always heard about the importance of rest, but it was typically framed as something you earned after six hard days of work. A reward for the productive. A prize for the worthy.

But God's design for rest was a rhythm sewn into the fabric of creation itself. Maybe the struggle wasn't about whether I could rest, but whether I was willing to. Would I sit still long enough to notice my breathing without immediately filling the silence with productivity?

Looking around me, metaphors were everywhere. Parts of the pilgrimage felt timeless, unchanged through centuries—the basic act of putting one foot in front of the other, the seeking, the longing for something more. Yet so much had evolved. Medieval pilgrims walked out of necessity and devotion, often barefoot, carrying almost nothing. I walked by choice, with lightweight gear, sturdy shoes, and a smartphone!

I needed to unpack what my understanding of pilgrimage actually was up to this point. *Why do I care so much about doing it "right"? What is a pilgrimage, really?* There was no committee grading my performance, no scorecard tracking my suffering. And yet I carried these invisible rules, these unspoken expectations, like stones in my pack.

I knew I was getting to the point where I needed to book a return ticket home. *Concrete plans. Blagh.* Back at our hotel, I pulled out my phone and started searching for flights, feeling that familiar tug between wanting to extend this trip forever and knowing I'd eventually need to return to real life. Whatever that meant.

I found a ticket from Santiago with a layover in Dublin and made an impulsive decision—why not give myself a whole day there? *One more city, one more adventure.* I booked the flight for May 15, even though I was pretty sure I'd reach Santiago almost a week before then. Better to have breathing room than to be scrambling at the end, right? I booked it before I could second-guess myself.

That was the extent of my planning for the rest of the day. I felt both settled and excited at the same time—a surprisingly pleasant combination.

Kathrine and I went out for dinner, and I ate a calamari sandwich the size of my face. It was golden-fried and perfectly crispy, served on crusty bread that required both hands and absolutely no dignity to eat. *Worth it.* The streets ebbed and flowed with people watching Semana Santa processions, others gearing up for a weekend of clubbing, and pilgrims lingering over bottles of wine with new friends.

We eventually found Leo and Ella, a pilgrim from The Netherlands, in a beautiful but surprisingly quiet square. I loved how the pastel-colored buildings—soft yellows, dusty pinks, pale blues—transformed into something almost jeweled in the combination of moonlight and street lamps. The plaza had a vintage-looking carousel in its center, complete with ornately colored horses, frozen mid-gallop and twinkling lights wrapped around the canopy. It gave the whole place a whimsical, joyful personality—like an elderly gentleman treating himself to an ice cream cone with sprinkles, completely unashamed of choosing joy.

Resting in Burgos, it was almost as if a switch in my brain got turned on—or maybe more accurately, like a door I'd been keeping carefully shut had finally swung open. A benefit of actually stopping and reflecting.

*9*

# Desert Mother

I did not want to leave Burgos. But the Way doesn't pause for anyone's reluctance, and soon Kathrine and I were back on the trail, the city shrinking behind us.

The contrast was immediate and almost comical. The ground beneath our feet shifted from smooth cobblestones to dirt mingled with broken tiles and loose gravel. It was a hot day, and within an hour gnats swarmed us. Not just a few annoying ones, but clouds of them invading our personal space with fervor. We must have looked like Pigpen from Charlie Brown, shuffling along in our own personal dust storms with insects orbiting our heads.

You would never have guessed we were coming from two days of somewhat polished hotel living and eating decadent meals. Now we were swatting bugs, wiping sweat from our foreheads, and negotiating with our blistered feet. The whiplash between the two realities: cathedral wonder and gnat-infested trudging, would have been absurd if it weren't so perfectly representative of this entire journey.

Beautiful one moment. Miserable the next. Pain and peace, all tangled together.

This stretch of the Camino is called the Meseta—180 kilometers of unvarying plains with nowhere to hide from the sun. It's been years since I walked on the Meseta, and I didn't know it then, but that flat land and vacant sky would be a grounding visual for me still to this day. I hate how easily I get distracted by small things and how quickly my day can get derailed by outside influences. So, though I am writing this while sitting at my dining table on a rainy Sunday after another hectic week, I am drawing my mind to the sunny April days walking in tandem with spring.

As a writer, there are few tasks that intimidate me more than approaching a blank page. Staring at the white sheet, I feel immense pressure to fill it with something worthy of taking up space. I look to the things that inspire me, and before I know it, my mind is filled with other people's words and concepts. I then have to sift through the swirl of ideas in my mind to find something that looks like it belongs to me. Ironically, I crave the blank page to allow my imagination to stretch and move in its own way, apart from the confluence of suggestions that I eagerly sought to "help" me.

The Meseta was my blank page. After resting and enjoying the beauty of Burgos, I found some much needed wiggle room on the trail for my mind and body. The flatter surface gave my knee a rest from the undulating terrain, and that allowed my thoughts to go from, *Ow, ow, ow, ow,* to, *that cloud looks like a turtle,* and *I wonder what is growing in that field...*

My mind could wander without being distracted by climbing or descending as it had been for the past couple of weeks. Though I still had knee pain, it wasn't enough to keep me from enjoying the musings that danced through my imagination as I wandered through fields in bloom. Before leaving for the Camino, I had read about the Desert Fathers and Mothers—those early Christian elders who'd fled to the wilderness to seek God away from the noise and distraction of the world. I'd think, *Why on earth would you intentionally go to the desert?* It seemed extreme. Unnecessary. Maybe even a little dramatic.

But here I was, in my version of the desert—stripped of my usual routines, my job titles, my carefully constructed identity—and I'd stumbled into an oasis I hadn't been looking for. Burgos had caught me off guard with its beauty, its rest, its invitation to simply *be.*

How much of a lesson is it, really, if we can fully anticipate the outcome? I didn't know what that time in Burgos would do for my soul. From the outside looking in, it probably just looked like someone drinking too much coffee and eating pastries in socks and sandals. *Peak tourist behavior.* But something was shifting inside me. The internal fidgeting that I seemed to feel at all times—that constant hum of anxiety, the mental list-making, the perpetual sense that I should be doing more—had slowed to a quieter rhythm.

And I felt lighter.

Laughing with Kathrine, I felt lighter. Walking through the cathedral with tears in my eyes, I felt lighter. Sitting in that square watching the carousel spin, I felt lighter. Being still—truly still, without guilt or agenda—I felt lighter.

Maybe the desert wasn't about deprivation after all. Maybe it was about making space for something I'd been too busy to notice before.

I thought I had a pretty good idea of what I was going to get out of the Camino. I think God was just going, "That's cute, but you're way off." The green plains kept my mind whirling with questions like, *Why am I really here? What do I do when I get home? Am I a true pilgrim? What is my purpose?* And then, blessedly, times when there was radio silence. I was listening to the breeze passing through the trees, the rhythm of my footsteps, the sound of trickling water, or the murmur of other pilgrims chatting on the trail.

Some days were hot and bug-filled. Others were cool and breezy. I got into the habit of taking regular breaks, either for my knee or to have a snack. Injuries can feel like setbacks or even straitjackets, but I couldn't get past the feeling that mine was a gift. The pain had become familiar, something I'd grown accustomed to and accepted as part of my pilgrimage. Because of my injury, I'd gained a new friend to walk with. No longer rushing with my head down, just trying to keep up, I was finally taking in my surroundings.

The best part of this was that I was given space for God to speak without even realizing it. In the melody of nature and the steadiness of my breathing. And it wasn't as though the words he spoke were great proclamations of purpose and direction; it felt like I was catching up with an old friend.

Kathrine and I were also in a comfortable place in our friendship where we could walk in silence or with headphones and not feel ignored. We took it easy with our pace and with our interactions.

My mind wandered as the kilometers passed, and I thought about things I hadn't considered in months. Small things. Simple things. The joy of having paint under my fingernails, for instance. I honestly love that feeling—love making things, getting messy in creativity, even if I never show the finished product to anyone. I am, if nothing else, just a crafty person. One of the jobs I had just quit was as a painter, but it had lost its luster long before I'd finally walked away. I painted rooms mostly— walls, trim, the occasional ceiling—which sounds artistic until you realize how incredibly mundane it actually is. And more often than not, gray was the color of choice. *Greige. Dove. Slate. Pewter.* All variations on the same soul-sucking neutral. It turns out there's a difference between making art and making things look acceptable for resale. One feeds your soul. The other just pays the bills.

I crave wonder, but I am delightfully surprised by whimsy. Little nuggets of light in dusty, dry places. Colors dancing on colorless plains designed by imagination and fueled by the desire for magic. *Hoppipolla* by Sigur Rós playing in the background.

Out there on the Meseta, disconnected from the noise of constant notifications and the pressure of social media, small pleasures became magnified. Simple activities felt meaningful. Simple foods tasted better. I only had texting and calls when I found Wi-Fi, and even that felt like plenty—maybe too much. The space between messages gave me room to think, to notice, to let my imagination roam without immediately capturing and curating it for an audience.

Maybe that's what I'd been missing: the freedom to create without performing, to be present without documenting, to let thoughts unfold without immediately knowing where they were headed. Many other pilgrims found this part of the Camino to be boring—the flat, repetitive landscape wearing on them—but I was really enjoying it. The steady rhythm, the open sky, the simplicity of just walking. That is, until the gluten I had consumed with reckless abandon in Burgos decided to fight back. Apparently, my body had not forgotten about my food sensitivities, even if I had. *Those pastries were so worth it at the time. Less worth it now.*

Arriving in Rabé de las Calzadas, I gave my stomach some time to recover and then dragged myself into a small cafe and, with absolutely no expectations, asked if they had anything gluten-free. The man behind the counter didn't even hesitate.

"Of course we have gluten-free food," he said, as if I'd insulted him by suggesting otherwise. "Go sit outside, and I will bring it to you."

*Okay then.* I obeyed, settling into a chair in the shade and waiting for my mystery dinner. Twenty minutes later, he appeared with a plate of crispy bacon and thick slices of chorizo sausage.

Voilà. Gluten-free.

After finishing my meat plate, I took a hot shower, hoping to burn away the bacon grease and any bugs that may have tried to set up camp in my hair. Detoxed and de-bugged, I settled into my bunk feeling cozy and content. In my journal that night, instead of just relaying the events of the day, I saved a few pages for a story that had started to formulate in my mind as I walked. I didn't know where I was going with it or if I would ever add to it—it was just nice to have the mental capacity to chew on something creative again. Characters seemed to sprout out of the ground somewhere along the trail.

The next day, however, did not share in the whimsical musings of the previous one. It was hot. It was long. And any creativity I'd felt the day before had evaporated along with my patience.

Hontanas was supposed to be our destination, but *where was this town?* We kept passing signs promising its arrival, but every time I looked to the horizon, there was nothing. Just more flat, endless plains. I was sweaty, surrounded by bugs, and I'm pretty sure I saw a mirage or two.

Then suddenly, the ground dropped away, and there it was: Hontanas, nestled in a freaking ravine like it had been hiding from us the whole time. The town was cute as anything—all amber-toned stone and terracotta roofs tucked into the hillside—but I was still mad about it. *You could've announced yourself sooner,* I thought bitterly as we descended into the village.

Our albergue was really cute, too. Looking newly renovated, the building had tall wooden ceilings with exposed beams. Each window seemed to frame a perfect picture of the surrounding buildings. AND it had a bar and restaurant, so we wouldn't have to wander around for food. *Thank you, Jesus.*

Kathrine and I sat outside at one of the tables spread out across the lawn with a jug of sangria and reveled in the sunset that seemed to be just for us. It's funny how easily I forgot the frustration I felt only a couple of hours before. And just as they had the previous night, the threads of my Meseta musings found their way into my journal before I drifted off to sleep.

What was it about this place? Each day I walked the Meseta, I swallowed a hundred flies, sweated through every layer, and my knee still ached. BUT by the time I climbed into my bunk, I had two or three pages of scenes and scenarios taking up space in my journal.

The next day, walking to Castrojeriz felt like a gift. I was feeling strong. Much stronger than I had since Los Arcos. We walked nine and a half kilometers in two and a half hours, which was the fastest I had gone in almost two weeks. I listened to an audiobook and imagined the story unfolding in the empty fields around me. I think I understood better why the Desert Fathers and Mothers had sought barren places—not because they were punishing themselves, but because emptiness creates room. Room to think, to pray, to let stories and ideas breathe without the constant noise of the world crowding them out.

We walked through the ruins of the Monastery of San Anton right as a tour bus pulled up to the site. Kathrine and I casually stopped for a snack not too far from the group so that we could shamelessly eavesdrop on the guide's history lesson.

Castrojeriz wasn't much farther beyond that, and as we approached, the lane leading into the city became lined with blossoming trees—their scent so sweet and heady it made me want to close my eyes and stay suspended in that moment forever. Which, considering I was walking along the side of a road, probably wasn't the safest impulse. But it was dreamy enough to make me consider the risk.

*10*

# Chasing Sunsets

The Castillo de Castrojeriz watched us from a distance as we made our way closer to our stop for the night, a silent sentinel perched atop a tall hill overlooking the Meseta. There's something both comforting and slightly unnerving about being observed by centuries-old ruins—like the land itself is noting your passage. *I'm just glad I don't have to climb up there.*

Before entering the town, Kathrine and I stopped at the Iglesia Colegiata de Nuestra Señora del Manzano, or Our Lady of the Apple Tree. The church stands on the site where it is said the Virgin Mary appeared to St. James beside an apple orchard. The church's foundations date back to around the 11th century, with multiple additions layered on through the centuries that followed, each generation leaving its mark. It functioned more like a museum than an active place of worship, filled with carefully curated exhibits and artifacts behind glass. Still, it was a beautiful space to wander through, and there was something remarkable about encountering so many layers of history in just one place.

After our time in the church, we walked into the honey-colored town, its medieval stone buildings glowing warmly in the afternoon light. We found our albergue, and I immediately felt relaxed. It was so inviting with its wonderfully eclectic decor—the kind of place where nothing quite matched, but somehow it all worked together. The tile flooring changed color and pattern every three feet or so, like walking through a patchwork quilt. It was quiet and cozy in a way that made you want to kick off your boots and stay a while.

The whole town radiated that same warmth and invitation, wrapping around us like a well-worn blanket.

Well, most of it, anyway.

A fellow pilgrim, Kathrine and I met, recommended that we go to the "silent albergue". An eclectic oasis for pilgrims to meditate and re-center. Kathrine and I took turns walking through the weathered building. Walls with faded paint and creaking floors housed a motley collection of paintings and sculptures. Worn furniture and scattered cushions provided spaces for visitors to sit and reflect. I was told I would find peace and serenity there. What I found instead? The heebies and the jeebies. This was the only time on the Camino I felt genuinely unsettled. That small vein carrying my Salvation Army blood must have burst, because I suddenly wished I had a tambourine and a Bible on hand. You were supposed to remain silent, but that didn't stop me from quietly humming "Nothing But the Blood" while running through every name of God I could remember.

Don't get me wrong; some rooms were genuinely beautiful, and I found the art refreshingly original. But peaceful? Not quite. Spooky? Yes. There was something in my spirit that was fighting the atmosphere of this place. It didn't help that I wasn't in there alone and didn't realize until I heard someone close behind me whisper, "Isn't it beautiful?" *AAAAHH!!!*

Kathrine and I were detoxing from the haunted house experience over a dinner of chicken wings and pizza when my Camino nephew, Leo, bounded up to invite us to watch the sunset with him and a few other pilgrims. We said yes before he told us it would be at the top of the citadel ruins. We hesitated.

This was the first day I'd actually felt stronger on the trail. Did I really want to jeopardize that newfound vitality by hauling myself up a steep hill for kicks? But then again, how fun would it be? And what was my alternative—sitting in the albergue twiddling my thumbs while everyone else went out to enjoy the night? *Again.*

I love a good jolt of adrenaline; I just find that as the time between jolts gets longer and longer; I worry I've become boring. I first felt it creeping in when I was a youth director in my mid-twenties. Watching my junior high students do cartwheels in the grass by the church, a sharp pang of jealousy struck me at the reckless abandon with which they hurled themselves over the ground. It looked like pure joy, but all I could think was that if I attempted a cartwheel, one of those students would need to drive me to the hospital.

As I write this chapter, I'm in training for a half-marathon. That's right—I'm a runner now. Just kidding. That statement has never been true, nor will it ever be. I have always been and will always be a walker.

In training for this half-marathon, I'm finding it remarkably difficult to stay motivated to move. Only on group run days do I actually meet my quota, which makes me think about the Camino and its curious blend of independence and dependence. What changes when we walk alone versus as a group? Well, my group was climbing up to the castle, so naturally, I was too. I returned to the albergue to get my walking poles because, even though I was willing, I didn't entirely think I was able.

It was different with Leo since he was considerably younger, but I felt a twinge of envy whenever other pilgrims my age—or older—managed to stand up without producing an involuntary sound effect. You know the one. That little grunt that announces to everyone within earshot that your joints have opinions about your life choices.

The trek up the hill wasn't nearly as arduous as I'd been bracing myself for—mostly because Kathrine kept us all in stitches with her running commentary on the absurdity of a late-night hike. Leo, bounding ahead with the inexhaustible energy of youth, would impatiently tease her about her pace, and she'd fire back with exactly what he could do with his impatience. Her retorts had me laughing so hard I forgot I was climbing.

When we finally reached the top, it felt absolutely triumphant. The ruins sprawled before us, with dimly lit platforms we could walk across to see the aged stonework up close. But the best view was looking down on Castrojeriz as lights began popping on in the streets below. The landscape stretched out around us in gentle hills and endless horizons—the kind of view that makes you feel both impossibly small and deeply connected to something larger.

The view, the company, the golden hour light—it was all picture perfect. And then reality came in to crash the party.

"What time is it?" I heard someone ask casually.

"9:25," another voice answered.

Kathrine and I locked eyes. Our albergue locked its doors at 9:30.

In my memory of that night, we were absolutely sprinting back down that mountain like our lives depended on it. Though, given our injuries and general physical limitations, I'm not sure "sprinting" is the right term. Let's call it "mangled speed-walking." All I know is that somehow—through sheer determination and possible divine intervention—we made it down that near vertical descent, past the locals enjoying their evening meals, and through our albergue doors at 9:40.

The host was kind enough to have kept the doors open for us, and we were profoundly, breathlessly grateful. Nothing says "spiritual pilgrimage" quite like nearly getting locked out because you were chasing a sunset.

The next day brought Easter morning, and while I thought we could start it off with a traditional Spanish Easter service, it turned out the service wasn't until the afternoon. *The trail it is then.* Though the Meseta is flatter than other parts of the Camino, some areas have varied topography. Such as Castrojeriz. The hill that held the castle ruins would not be the only one I climbed that weekend. Just as you exit the town, you head towards a cluster of hills that I was really wishing the trail went around and not over.

My wish was not granted.

At least the weather was cooperating. It was sunny but not oppressively hot yet, and the breeze was gentle—more of a companion than an adversary as I slowly made my way up the steep climb of Alto de Mostelares. Since we'd left at different times that morning, I didn't have Kathrine's hilarious commentary to distract me from the ascent, but I didn't mind. I was focused and determined. *I'm making it to the top.*

I didn't expect to get emotional when I got there, but I did. This was the hardest climb I'd tackled since injuring my knee, and I'd actually done it. I found a spot along the old stone wall that runs along the edge of the hilltop and used it as a backrest, letting myself just sit for a moment. I peeled a clementine and looked out over the ground I had covered, and gratitude swept over me like a wave. My knee was sore from the increased exertion—I could feel it protesting—but maybe because it was Easter, I felt grace that reached beyond the pain.

Kathrine joined me at my spot, and we both felt immense pride that we had made it this far, despite the setbacks. What a gift. Speaking of gifts, we eventually met up with James, Leo, Ella, a few others, and received some Easter chocolates. *Could this day get any better?* Yes, it could. That night at the albergue in Itero de la Vega, I got a little taste of home. Ketchup chips.

The next day I walked twenty-seven kilometers—by accident.

The most interesting relationship I experienced while walking the Camino was undoubtedly with my guidebook. I loved the information and history it provided, but I had some trust issues with the stages it suggested. There are multiple guidebooks on the Camino, and they will all give you slightly different experiences. A friend gifted me one shortly before I left, and I was thrilled to have this wisdom guiding my journey.

At first, I wouldn't let this book out of my sight. Any moment of confusion or pause? Consult the guidebook. Unsure about a Spanish custom or tradition? Out comes the guidebook. I believed this book was everything I could possibly need to make my Camino as smooth as possible.

Well. That was optimistic.

This book would eventually become my nemesis. On this day, it actually caused me physical pain! (No, not a paper cut.)

I was walking separately from Kathrine and was due to meet her in the town of Villarmentero de Campos. According to my paperback boyfriend, I could take a highway path or a scenic river path—both would lead to my destination. I chose the river path and walked right past the town we were supposed to be staying in and just kept going, all the while thinking, *I'm pretty sure I missed it...* I had. By about eight kilometers. *Oops.* The markers I was supposed to watch out for were either not there or very well hidden. That miscommunication put a real strain on our relationship, and I couldn't help but read the directions that followed with considerable suspicion. I wasn't alone.

Pilgrims would gather around cafe tables comparing notes like couples in therapy: "Mine said I should walk thirty-five kilometers tomorrow!"

"Well, *mine* didn't mention any of the albergues here!"

"I haven't had any issues with mine so far." Everyone at the table would turn and stare. The pilgrim continued in hushed tones, "Okay, well, sometimes I wonder if mine thinks I have all the time in the world, because it keeps suggesting I visit every off-trail attraction."

Despite their quirks and frustrations, guidebooks are invaluable. We walked past many beautiful landmarks and structures with no signs, but our books preserved their stories. They offer tips on terrain and weather, but most importantly, they have a map tucked in their back pocket—and sometimes, that's everything.

Luckily, when I reached Villalcázar de Sirga, I ran into Anne, whom I'd met back in Hontanas. She graciously got me into the nice hostel where she was staying. Kathrine followed shortly after by taxi, more than happy to abandon the decidedly creepy albergue we'd originally booked. She had stories. By the end of it all, I was sore and exhausted, but genuinely happy I'd pushed that far. It was beautiful. It was long. And my guidebook and I were officially on a break.

*11*

# Stroopwafels in the Shire

We woke to cloudy skies, and scattered rain showers threatening overhead. We walked six kilometers to Carrión de los Condes, then settled in to wait for the bus that would take us to Terradillos de los Templarios.

I'd often worried about the judgment we might receive for taking the bus, but I was realizing that criticism existed mainly in my head. There were plenty of other pilgrims waiting at the bus stop with us—the forecast had called for heavier rain and wind, and people were making practical choices. *It's the Way, not the Walk...*

There was a distinct feeling in the air around this point on the Camino. Maybe it was because we were approaching the halfway mark, but there seemed to be a growing need among pilgrims to compare notes—to know everyone's pace, when they started, and how far they walked each day. *Why* they started felt like it was getting lost in all the logistics. It was beginning to feel less like a shared experience and more like a competition.

Well, part of my experience was busting my knee a few days in, and speaking of which—I may have been feeling a little overconfident that day. After successfully climbing that hill in Castrojeriz, Alto de Mostelares and logging twenty-seven kilometers to Villalcázar de Sirga, I was practically strutting. So naturally, in my moment of triumph, I got off the bus a little too quickly and shocked my knee on the way down. Pain shot through it immediately, a sharp reminder that I wasn't nearly as far along my recovery journey as I'd foolishly assumed.

We had a filling meal at the albergue that night and got reunited with our Finnish friend Hannu, which lifted our spirits considerably. Leo, Ella, and I stumbled upon an actual Juego de la Oca (The Goose Game) box set and tried our hand at the board game, though none of us really understood the rules. The combination of heavy food and gloomy weather had me ready for bed earlier than normal.

My room had six or seven single beds spread around instead of the standard bunks we'd grown accustomed to—a pleasant change of pace. I was certain I would sleep heavily that night.

If it weren't for the Portuguese woman whispering in my ear all night long.

She wasn't *technically* whispering in my ear, mind you, but the strange acoustics in that room created some kind of sound tunnel. I could clearly hear every mumble, murmur, and nocturnal commentary this woman produced in her sleep from the opposite corner of the room. It was like having surround sound for someone else's dreams.

The next day couldn't have been more different. My legs were sore, but I couldn't help enjoying the day because it was like walking straight through Middle Earth. The sunshine was warm and bright. The lush green fields rolled out before us like The Shire itself, complete with hobbit-like holes (bodegas, actually) peeking out from the ground. I listened to some of Howard Shore's score from the movies as I slowly meandered around the mounds, hoping to bump into Merry and Pippin.

My breakfast stop that morning included something that made me smile—peanut butter! Happily fed and slightly giddy, I left the restaurant, hoping the story idea I'd started earlier on the Meseta might join me in The Shire.

Walking through Moratinos was a whimsical delight as many of the trees in town were wearing sweaters. Brightly colored crocheted bunting draped from branches and wrapped around trunks, adding to my overall impression that I'd somehow walked straight into a storybook. San Nicolás del Camino Real wasn't far beyond that, and though breakfast hadn't been that long before, we stopped for some fresh orange juice. I wanted to linger in this fantastical realm a little while longer.

Because even though the atmosphere was warm and beautiful—magical, really—my body was hurting. Weeks of walking, climbing, sleeping in different beds, and carrying a backpack, all while my legs tried desperately to recover, were really wearing on me.

I don't think anyone has ever described me as being "light on my feet." I'm kind of built like a hockey player—solid, grounded, not exactly graceful. After hurting my knee, I felt even clunkier when I walked. I was Samwise Gamgee carrying all the pots and pans, except it was my own injured limbs that felt like the clanging cargo. What I wanted, desperately, was to be Legolas—gliding delicately across the top of snow without leaving so much as a footprint.

*Lord of the Rings* references aside, I found it genuinely difficult not to compare my physical condition with everyone around me. Some pilgrims seemed to bounce along the trail with endless energy, their legs like springs rather than bone and muscle. They made it look effortless. I made it look like a project.

And yet, despite the soreness, I kept moving forward. One foot in front of the other, day after day. Which is how I eventually found myself standing before two large statues marking the halfway point—positioned, I couldn't help but notice, much like the ones at the end of *The Fellowship of the Ring*. (Sorry, one more *LOTR* reference...)

Halfway.

I sat down and just stared at those monuments for a long while, letting the reality settle over me. It's a strange feeling to reach a midpoint—relief and sadness arriving at the same time, tangled together. Those past three weeks, though painful, had been some of the happiest of my life. I wanted to hold on to all of it: the beauty of the landscape, the quiet, the unexpected companionship. But I also knew that limbo has a time limit. At some point, the real world would be waiting.

I didn't think I'd be excited about that. But I actually was.

I'm at my most restless when I don't have something to look forward to. A close second is being stuck in between, in the middle—neither here nor there, just suspended in space.

This pilgrimage, though set in Spain, felt like its own kind of no-man's-land. I was so far removed from day-to-day activities and "regular" life that it created a strange headspace, one that felt both freeing and disorienting at the same time.

I sat and stared at those halfway statues, knowing that eventually I'd have to stand up and walk through them, past them, beyond them. Part of me wanted to freeze this moment, to live here in the middle where anything still felt possible.

If only I could see all in-betweens like that, as places of potential rather than paralysis. I got up from the halfway marker, brushed off my pants, and made my way into Sahagún, though my mind was still sitting back there with those statues.

One of my favorite dishes I'd discovered on the Camino was *patatas bravas*, garlicky potatoes swimming in a spicy tomato sauce. And it's gluten-free! The *patatas bravas* I had in Sahagún were hands-down the most garlicky I'd encountered yet.

No matter how much I brushed my teeth or scrubbed my skin in the shower afterward, I still reeked of garlic. It was radiating from my pores. I smelled like I could single-handedly ward off an entire coven of vampires.

It was too early to check into the albergue, so Katherine and I ambled through Sahagún's streets, waiting for the garlic odor to disappear. Thankfully, the smell faded as we walked, and a much more enticing smell soon replaced it, drifting through the air.

Kathrine and I both stopped mid-stride, lifted our noses, and started sniffing like bloodhounds. The sweet aroma led us down a narrow street and in front of a tiny bakery selling stroopwafels—a traditionally Dutch delicacy comprising thin waffles filled with honey or caramel.

Two women were working behind the counter, and they'd just finished making a large batch of freshly baked treats, still radiating warmth. They handed Kathrine and me each a warm stroopwafel as a sample, and before they could even finish asking if we wanted to buy a bag, we were already nodding enthusiastically.

Reflection is an inevitable part of being in the middle—there's no escaping it when you're suspended between where you've been and where you're going. That night I lay in my bunk, unable to sleep, and thought back over the past three weeks. The expectations I'd carried before beginning, the physical toll of the trail, the goals I'd wanted to reach, my faith journey, the landscape, the lessons. And most of all, the people I'd met.

The people.

Kathrine in particular.

I am seven years her senior, but it never felt like that. On this trail, we met each other as equals, both of us figuring things out as we went. Remarkably self-sufficient and endlessly curious—that was Kathrine, two of my very favorite things about her. She had a knack for engaging with everything, always being the first to ask names, seek directions when lost, or try new foods. Making sure we all got pictures together to remember the moments was another of her gifts. The Danish phrases she taught me, I absolutely butchered, but she got such a kick out of my attempts that I kept trying anyway. I could not have wished for a better person to walk beside through all of this.

As far as "in-betweens" go, I had to admit—I liked this one. I know I'd been hoping to be struck by lightning-bolt epiphanies and clear life-directions by this halfway point. But God knows what he's doing when he asks us to wait, to sit in the uncertainty a little longer. I found myself caught between a life of hectic schedules I'd never fully surrendered and God's brilliant unknown stretching out ahead of me.

And maybe, for now, that was exactly where I needed to be.

Kathrine and I spent the next day chatting and laughing about everything and nothing as we walked. Despite our exhaustion and soreness, it was a beautiful, sunny day, and we were determined to enjoy it together.

That day turned into a sort of friendship validation day without us planning it. We kept running into other pilgrims, and they'd ask how we knew each other, so we got to share the story of our meeting over and over.

More people asked us why we were there, what had brought us to the Camino, and there was something renewing about articulating it repeatedly. Though I felt significant pain radiating through my legs with every step, my soul felt like it was healing.

We met a pilgrim at a cafe who gave us a great recommendation for our upcoming rest days in León.

"Take yourselves to the movies," he said with a knowing smile. "That's a great way to force yourselves to actually stop and rest. Otherwise, you'll just keep wandering around the city on tired legs."

We chatted with him a while longer, and he shared that he was losing his eyesight. He was deliberately traveling the world now, taking full advantage of the time he had left before blindness fully set in. The weight of that hit me hard. How many of us would prioritize resting if we knew we had limited time to see the world around us? Yet here was this man, choosing to sit in a dark theater, to give his body the rest it needed, even as his vision faded.

I searched his face and found contentment there—genuine peace, even amid profound loss.

*So glad I'm wearing my sunglasses right now so no one can see me welling up but, dang it, I'm going to the movies!*

A couple of Australian *hospitaleros* (volunteer hosts), who showered all of us weary pilgrims with genuine kindness, ran our albergue in El Burgo Ranero. There are some people you can just tell, simply by their smile, that they give good hugs. These two had that quality in spades.

As soon as we stepped through the door, before we could even set down our packs, someone offered us hot chocolate and biscuits. Not as an afterthought, but as a welcome—like we were guests arriving home rather than strangers passing through.

Our hosts had a tradition of gathering their guests into a circle each evening. It was a chance for all of us to connect, to pause from the constant forward motion and actually absorb one another's experiences. The hospitaleros brought a poem about walking. They translated it into many languages so our diverse group of pilgrims could hear it in their own tongues.

As we went around the circle, my mind drifted unexpectedly to the tape markers on the floor at work—those strips of vinyl reminding us all to keep our distance. Covid wasn't completely gone, but we had better precautions in place now. But there was something about this night, this gathering, that made me acutely aware of how separate we'd all been for the past two years. How we feared company, dreaded proximity, and saw other humans as potential threats.

Not here. Here we sat shoulder to shoulder, passing a poem between us like a sacred thing.

That room likely held people with opposing political and cultural views. Their beliefs probably clashed, and they might not normally seek each other's company. But it didn't matter. We shared the road. We'd walked the same path, felt the same blisters, carried the same weight. That was enough.

After the poetry reading, our hosts suggested we all walk together to watch the sunset. No one hesitated.

As a group, we followed them out to a wide-open view where the sky was already beginning to turn colors. I looked around at this pack of pilgrims—people from different countries, of different ages, different lives entirely—all standing quietly, watching the sky together.

And here's what struck me: I don't remember seeing phones out to capture the moment. No one was frantically angling for the perfect shot. We were just... there. Witnessing this simple joy together.

## 12

# You Get What You Give

"Today is not a day for walking."

I turned to see a Norwegian mountain man from our albergue standing beside us. He positioned himself under the weathered awning next to Kathrine and me as we waited for the bus, rain drumming steadily on the canvas above our heads. Previously, when I took the bus, unnecessary shame had weighed down my mind; this shame stemmed from snippy comments from judgmental pilgrims, or more likely, from my own relentless self-deprecation, which told me I wasn't doing the Camino "right."

But this morning, standing in the rain with aching legs and heavy eyelids, I didn't care. I was absolutely beat, and the large, imposing man next to me, who was on his *ninth* Camino and clearly had nothing left to prove, was taking the bus too. If someone who'd walked this path eight times before could give himself permission to rest, then so could I.

Despite the beauty of the previous night's communal poetry gathering, I hadn't slept well. My mind had been too full, or perhaps my body too sore, probably both. I was more than happy to spend this rainy morning on a bus, watching the landscape blur past through rain-streaked windows instead of trudging through it step by painful step.

León would be our stop for the next three days.

After arriving at the bus station in León, we walked quietly towards the center of town. The cathedral was in our sight, but our eyes drifted to a lit "COFFEE" sign, and our feet changed course. In an almost zombie-like state, we walked into this cafe and unloaded our heavy layers. We ordered our coffees and some breakfast while subtly bobbing our heads to the familiar tunes playing on the radio. When ordering coffee in Europe, many places will give you a little complimentary treat, like chocolate or a biscuit, along with your drink. This cafe gave us donuts. I was already in a state of weariness and apathy, so, you know, I wasn't going to think twice about eating the chunk of gluten in front of me.

I was mumbling along to "You Get What You Give" by New Radicals when I took my first bite. Then something unexpected happened. I began to cry. That crazy combination of exhaustion, nostalgic alt rock, forbidden desserts, and a rainy morning made a cocktail of an emotion for which I have no name. I looked over at Kathrine and she was crying too. We needed these rest days more than I thought.

Kathrine and I had booked separate places to stay for that first night, then planned to share a *pensione* for the following two days. I found the albergue I'd reserved that night after many twists and turns in the labyrinth of alleyways and side streets that make up León. From the outside, it wasn't particularly distinctive—just another weathered door in an ancient stone wall. But the moment I stepped inside, I was met by bright lights and furniture practically dripping with color.

There was a communal kitchen, a well-stocked coffee and tea station, and several tables surrounded by cheerful bar stools. I made my way to the freezer and stashed a knee ice pack I'd bought en route. In the center of the hostel was an atrium with bistro tables and chairs arranged around a single tree dressed in fairy lights. The effect was magical, almost dreamlike.

I lumbered my way up to the dorms and found my spacious bunk outfitted with fresh linens and privacy curtains. Have I mentioned the absolute luxury that is a bunk with curtains? It's the small things that feel monumental on the Camino.

After a blissfully hot shower, I wandered back down to the kitchen to make myself something to eat. That's when I discovered they had gluten-free cereal and dairy-free milk available for guests. *Am I dreaming?* I actually stood there staring at the shelf for a moment, convinced I was hallucinating from exhaustion.

After eating my cereal, I retrieved my ice pack from the freezer and headed back to my bunk, where I drew the privacy curtain and settled in for the night, cocooned in my own little sanctuary.

I slept for ten hours straight that night.

Looking back through my photos later, I found a selfie Kathrine had taken of us that morning at the bus stop: two bedraggled pilgrims with heavy eyelids and half-hearted smiles, barely holding it together.

The clouds still hung overhead the following morning, but they hadn't been filled with rain as they had the day before. Bitterly cold, but dry enough for the festivities of Castile y León Day. People were filling the streets to watch the parades of folk dancers and musicians commemorating the anniversary of the Battle of Villalar.

I spotted a shop with clothing stands displayed out front and made a beeline for it, weaving past a procession of pipers and color guard. The wind was cutting through my layers more fiercely than I'd expected, and I desperately needed something to shield my face. *Why didn't I pack a scarf? Oh, right, because I thought Spain would be warm in April.* I grabbed a fleece scarf and wrapped it around my neck immediately as I paid the shopkeeper, not even waiting to leave the store.

Still cold despite my new accessory, I headed to a nearby cafe for some proper fortification: coffee and churros con chocolate. *Worth it,* I thought as the server set down the plate of golden churros and a cup of thick, velvety chocolate. My dietary sensitivities required me to "minimize" gluten and dairy — a word, I was discovering, that is entirely open to interpretation. If you're going to have a little of something, make it churros con chocolate. I was halfway through a swan dive into my decidedly non-compliant breakfast when I heard a voice,

"Hello, Canadian girl."

I looked up to see a pilgrim from Germany I'd met shortly after meeting Kathrine. She stood there with a tentative smile, and I immediately gestured for her to join me. Her name was Tilde, and she had been absolutely through the wringer on the Camino. She'd battled Covid a couple of weeks earlier, and just when she'd recovered from that, vicious food poisoning had laid her low before arriving in León. She wore a brave face as she sat down, but I could see the weariness behind her eyes. *I bet she didn't expect anything like this from her pilgrimage.*

Even though I'd only met her briefly once before, I was glad she felt comfortable enough to come over and ask to join me for breakfast. We settled into an easy conversation, and it wasn't too long before Leo joined us as well, his energy infectious even in the sleepy morning light. Absolutely buzzing with excitement as he and his dad were planning on getting Camino tattoos while in

León. It was his first one, and he was practically counting down the minutes until they could get to the shop. I have several tattoos myself, so he peppered me with questions about aftercare, what to expect, and whether it would hurt as much as he thought. *Yes! I'm the cool aunt!* There was something sweet about his nervous excitement, that mix of anticipation and slight terror that comes with doing something new and irreversible.

As the day progressed, Kathrine and I dropped our backpacks off at our pensión, and I convinced her to take a couple of inches off my hair. The split ends and dryness from the constant exposure to sun and wind had made my wavy hair frizz and break—it was driving me nuts! A typical fresh haircut feels like clean sheet night. But on the Camino, it's downright dreamy. Was it even? No. Did I care? Not even a little.

I washed my freshly trimmed hair, reveling in how much lighter it felt, and Kathrine and I wandered leisurely through the shops in León's winding streets before meeting James and Leo for dinner. I found a small blue floral notebook at one store and decided that it was time to move the fictional story I had worked on out of my journal and into a home of its own. Writing had become part of my nightly routine—scribbling a few lines before bed, even if the story was just for me. There was something freeing about creating something on the Camino that had nothing to do with the Camino itself.

James and Leo had us meet them at an Italian restaurant they had eaten at the previous night. They enjoyed the food so much that they were considering a third night there. I don't blame them; the food was delicious. (And had gluten-free options!)

By the time we finished our meal, it was dark out, and the Catedral de Santa Maria de León was just outside the door, glowing dramatically in the streetlights like something out of a fairytale. *Show-off,* I thought affectionately of the ancient building. We briefly met up with a couple of other pilgrims for drinks and dessert before making our way back to our accommodation.

I woke up early the next morning and took my new blue notebook into the common area and enjoyed some quiet time to myself. I made myself a cup of coffee and let my mind wander wherever it needed to on my new blank pages. It felt like I was working a muscle I had forgotten I had. I've always enjoyed scribbling away at little stories, but it had definitely been a while. I had graduated college with a degree in writing, full of hope and ambition, but after not finding work in that field, it became more of a hobby than a pursuit.

What I was finding in this mental stage of my Camino was that this hobby—this thing I'd relegated to the dusty shelf of backlogged dreams—was saving me from endless introspection and allowing my imagination to direct some of the mental steps instead. This small amount of scribbles that had become the bookend of my days now felt like a God-given gift. Not a distraction, not an escape, but something more essential than that. The Creator using creativity as a healing agent. Maybe all those blank pages were exactly what I needed—not another journal entry dissecting my feelings, but a place where something new could grow.

Though there was still something of a chill in the air, the sun was out! *Finally.* We took it slow in the morning, indulging in the luxury of not having anywhere we needed to be, no kilometers we needed to log. Kathrine and I wandered into Plaza de San Marcelo, where locals were already claiming benches and outdoor cafe tables, soaking up the rare warmth. We found a sunny spot and settled in with a mid-day glass of wine.

Leo met up with us soon after we arrived, his tattoo freshly wrapped and his grin even wider than usual. We began planning our afternoon with the casual enthusiasm of people who had all the time in the world.

On the advice of our friend back in El Burgo Ranero, we made our way to the closest movie theater to watch *The Lost City* featuring Sandra Bullock, Channing Tatum, and, mercifully, English subtitles. It was hilarious and utterly absurd and just what we needed.

The night found us back at the same Italian restaurant because, at this point, it had become a tradition. Afterward, the four of us stood outside gazing up at the cathedral, its illuminated spires reaching toward the night sky, and I felt something settle in my chest. Gratitude, maybe. Or just peace.

Looking back on those days now, I can fully see the benefit of resting for that long, even though at the time I had moments of restlessness as I watched other pilgrims shouldering their packs and continuing on without us. *Should I be walking? Am I falling behind?* But the Camino wasn't going anywhere.

At the beginning of my pilgrim journey, it was as though instead of my yellow backpack; I carried myself on my back—Dead-Weight Amy, who had been crawling out of her skin, disillusioned, burdened by unspoken stresses and anxieties I couldn't seem to name. She whispered self-doubt and harsh criticism in my ear whenever I stumbled, a relentless internal voice that refused to let me rest. I wanted nothing more than to shake her off, to leave her behind on the trail somewhere.

But as time went on, something shifted. I wasn't as heavy to carry anymore. The weight didn't disappear entirely—that would be too neat, too simple—but it redistributed somehow. Kathrine carried me for a while. I carried her. We took turns holding each other up, sometimes literally, sometimes just through presence and laughter, and shared silence.

And I was in no doubt that God was walking with me too, carrying me when I didn't even realize I needed carrying. Even when I felt like I wasn't able to focus on time with Him. He was there.

I'd spent so long trying to carry everything alone, convinced that needing help was weakness, that admitting struggle was failure. But on the Camino, I was learning that strength looks different than I thought. It looks like admitting you can't take another step. It looks like accepting a hand when it's offered.

Maybe Dead-Weight Amy wasn't something for me to shake off. Maybe she just needed to be held.

*13*

# Trout Soup

On the way out of León, I felt the top of my right foot tighten. A couple of hours into our walk, we stopped at a cafe and I indulged in a chorizo bocadillo (*I know, I know, more gluten. I'm rolling my eyes at myself at this point*) and requested an ice pack for my foot. The owner had plenty on hand, and I could relax my throbbing foot while I ate.

A combination of highway and gravel paths was not a bad way to re-acquaint ourselves with the road after our extended rest. The rhythm came back gradually, muscle memory taking over even as my legs protested. But it was far less aesthetically pleasing than what we'd grown used to. The Meseta stretched out in all directions, and the constant hum of traffic on the N-120 made it feel less like a pilgrimage and more like a very long, very dusty roadside march.

For pilgrims who grow weary of walking beside the highway and its endless parade of trucks, there's a detour—a quieter alternative that adds a few kilometers but trades the noise and exhaust for something more peaceful. Kathrine and I chose this route, making our way toward Villar de Mazarife, about twenty-one kilometers from León.

After three days of resting, lounging, wine-drinking, and movie-watching, my legs had clearly forgotten what they were supposed to be doing. Every muscle protested the reminder. The route was also poorly marked, and we found ourselves second-guessing each turn. Kathrine called James and Leo, who were somewhere ahead of us on the trail, and they talked us through the right path without hesitation—they'd wrestled with the same confusing stretch not long before.

I was going through my mental gymnastics routine—replaying the past few days of rest, second-guessing whether we'd stayed too long, wondering if my foot would hold up—when I stopped to look behind me to see how close Kathrine was. When I did, I saw something that made me catch my breath. In the far distance, snow-capped mountains lined the horizon, their peaks glowing softly in the daylight. Ahead of us were just more plains, brown and endless and ordinary. But behind us was a reminder of the beauty of what we had passed through, a landscape we'd conquered one step at a time without fully realizing it.

They were not the Pyrenees that we had crossed at the beginning; those felt like another lifetime now. We had journeyed just under 500 kilometers. About 310 miles. *We walked that. With our own feet. And a bus or two. On purpose.* It hit me then, standing there on that unremarkable dirt path, that we were doing something extraordinary, even on the days when it felt mundane or painful or pointless. The mountains behind us were proof.

We were walking along fields of cheerful yellow rapeseed and, after stopping to take some pictures of each other with a refreshingly bright background,

Kathrine and I surmised we might both be allergic to rapeseed. We took all the pictures between sneezes, and congestion joined me for the rest of the day.

My knees and my foot were throbbing and begging to be put up by the time we reached our albergue in Villar de Mazarife. *Just let me sit down. That's all I'm asking.* Conveniently, miraculously, even, our albergue had a masseuse on site! If I were anywhere else, I would not subject another human being to touching my feet, which at this point looked like they had gone through a meat grinder. But this man worked on the Camino with pilgrims regularly, so he knew exactly what he was up against. He'd probably seen worse. At least, that's what I told myself.

After my massage, I called my dad to chat for a bit, catching him up on León and the rest days and the bocadillos that were slowly destroying my digestive system. It was nice to hear his voice, to feel tethered to home for a few minutes, even though I was halfway across the world. Then I took a shower to wash off the day's sweat, dust, and potential allergens, standing under the lukewarm water longer than I probably should have.

As I toweled off, I caught myself wincing, not from my foot, but from the uncomfortable bloating that had become an unwelcome companion. *I really need to be more conscious of my gluten intake*, I thought, annoyed with myself.

The problem was that I was still so new to all of it. My intolerance had only recently come to light, and I hadn't yet developed a clear sense of what I could get away with and what would flatten me. Every time I ate something questionable, there was a moment of internal negotiation—a quiet, *maybe it'll be fine this time*—followed, inevitably, by the realization that it was not, in fact, fine. I also hated the idea of making a fuss. Walking into a small café in rural Spain and announcing my dietary needs felt like an imposition, and so more often than not, I simply didn't. When I was hungry and the only options were croissants and tortillas, I ate the croissants and tortillas and told myself I'd be more careful tomorrow.

It was hard not to resent it; this new limitation that had shown up uninvited, like an added tax on an already demanding journey. As if blisters and aching knees weren't enough.

I barely slept that night. Sore, bloated, and congested, I lay there like a grumpy balloon someone had over-inflated. Every position felt wrong. My back made my sinuses throb. My side made my hips ache. *This is miserable.* I wasn't looking forward to the next day of walking, but lying still didn't feel much better either.

I wished I'd had more time before coming to Spain—time to experiment, to map my own limits, to figure out the rules of this new body I apparently had. But even as the thought formed, I knew it was mostly self-pity. Probably nothing would have changed. *I'd still be here. Still bloated. Still stubborn.*

The following day, I filled my spare water bottle with ginger tea, hoping to get my gut back to a happy place. We walked fifteen kilometers to the medieval town of Hospital de Órbigo, where the detour route and the main trail finally met back up. To enter the town, we had to cross a beautiful stone bridge, the Puente del Paso Honroso, that arched gracefully over the river and overlooked a jousting tournament field. You read that right. A jousting field. In 2022. Each step across that ancient bridge seemed to pull us further and further into the past, the modern world slipping away behind us. *As long as the past includes a bed and ibuprofen, I don't mind one bit.*

All throughout this blast-from-the-past town were references to Don Suero, a 15th-century lovelorn knight who had regained his honor by holding and winning a tournament on this very spot before walking the Camino to Santiago. I genuinely wished I could see this tournament, which they apparently re-enact every summer, with knights in armor and swooning maidens.

We had walked on Roman roads and sat in centuries-old cathedrals, but Hospital de Órbigo was something else entirely. Though it looked locked in the 12th century, with all stone archways and narrow streets, it was full of amenities designed for 21st century pilgrims who still needed Wi-Fi and washing machines.

Kathrine and I found our albergue, which outwardly matched the medieval aesthetic perfectly but inwardly housed what I consider a modern miracle: individually curtained bunks. *Yeeesss.*

Kathrine and I practically tumbled into our beds, groaning with relief as we finally got off our feet. My foot and knee really throbbed with each heartbeat, and Kathrine's ankles painfully swelled. We were beat, completely and utterly done for the day.

Kathrine announced she was in for the night, and despite my exhaustion, I ventured out for dinner. *Maybe I'll find some wassail or a turkey leg or something.* I found a restaurant just down the cobblestone street that was packed with hungry pilgrims and settled into an empty seat.

The server, noticing my indecision as I stared blankly at the menu, leaned in and mentioned the region's trout soup, which was favored by pilgrims.

How does one describe "trout soup?" Well, I think "soup" might be a stretch. I love soup. It's probably my favorite kind of food. Nothing warms your bones quite like a good soup. I ate this soup with a fork. It's basically a whole loaf of bread and a fish with broth poured over the top, which the bread quickly soaks up. *Soup indeed.* I know I just wrote about trying to avoid bread, but in my defense, this one came at me unannounced!

I avoided the bread as best I could, as I had nearly recovered from the previous night's discomfort. The fish was warm and delicious, but I felt guilty about not cleaning the bowl after the server had hyped up the dish. I just couldn't handle any more gut drama.

I pulled out my phone and checked the Camino family WhatsApp group chat to find that Emilija had made it to Santiago earlier that day. I told you she could move. Here I was, exhausted and poking at a bowl of questionable "soup," every muscle in my body aching, and she had already finished. I genuinely don't know how she did it.

Emilija had been one of the first people I'd connected with on the trail. She was warm and funny and moved through the Camino with a kind of quiet ferocity that I admired. And now, just twenty-five days after setting out, her pilgrimage was complete, while mine still had a long road ahead.

I closed the app, set my phone face-down on the table, and pushed what was left of the soup around the bowl for a while longer. Then I slowly made my way back to my cozy bunk and conked out. No journal entries, no scribbles. Just out cold.

Kathrine informed me in the morning that she would take the bus to Astorga, as her ankles had improved little from the day before. I had had a solid night of sleep, and my body had detoxed from my dietary detours, so I was feeling strong enough for the trail. We would meet up later in Astorga for dinner.

This was my first time walking alone in weeks. Kathrine and I didn't always walk directly next to each other or talk the whole time, but we were together— within shouting distance, sharing the same rhythm, the same stops. Now, with her taking the bus, the path felt wider somehow, quieter. I decided I would record some video messages for my family as I walked, narrating the scenery and my thoughts like some kind of low-budget travel show. Kathrine had asked me to take pictures of the day she was missing out on, clearly frustrated that her body had benched her. So I threw in a few silly pictures to help ease that frustration and make her laugh.

Like in the early days on the Meseta, my mind took advantage of the open space around me to daydream, reflect, create, and pray. My thoughts drifted in and out without resistance, unforced and unhurried. I thought about Emilija. She was about to re-enter normal life while I was still out here, still walking, still becoming whatever this journey was making me. I wasn't jealous, exactly. More wistful. And if I'm honest, I was a little relieved that I still had time left.

I stopped for a snack under a shady tree and took a deep breath, closing my eyes. I wanted to remember the smell of the world around me—the open, fresh air, the earthy scent of rolling fields, and the wildflowers just starting to bloom. It would be nice if that were the only scent around me.

You can shower as much as you want on the Camino, but you can't escape the fragrance of pilgrimage. To be honest, I kind of liked it at first. Not in an "I hope this comes in a candle" kind of way, but it made the world I was living in feel more real, more lived-in. Toward the end of the Camino, however, I found myself fantasizing about a fresh, clean shirt. One that doesn't smell like a gym bag left in a car trunk for three weeks.

I had an insert that I'd added to my backpack before leaving, one of those organizational systems designed to help keep things tidy: pockets for socks, underwear, money, snacks, and a separate slot for dirty clothes. It did work in keeping things organized, technically. Everything had its place. But a few cloth sleeves were not nearly enough to keep the smell of the road from permeating every crevice of that bag, and by extension, me.

I had much more ground to cover, so I stopped sniffing the air like a weirdo and continued on. The terrain had become more varied as the León mountains rose on the horizon, their presence a welcome change from the endless flat Meseta. *Finally, something to look at besides dirt and sky.* I stopped one more time on my way to Astorga, and it was at La Casa de Los Dioses, a *donativo* rest stop that felt like stumbling into an oasis.

There were other pilgrims scattered around this colorful outpost, resting in whatever patch of shade they could claim. The hosts had laid out fruit, nuts, and crackers like offerings on low tables and tree stumps. A drink stand held varying pitchers of juice, tea, coffee, and milk. I helped myself to some dried apricots and almonds and made myself a coffee with coconut milk, grateful for options that wouldn't wreck my stomach. Though there were maybe ten other people at this shelter, it was quiet—not an awkward or heavy quiet, but a comfortable and contented one.

I could feel my painkillers wearing off, that familiar throb creeping back into my foot and knee, and I still had another eight kilometers to go. Great. Not wanting to break the silence, I threw back my coffee and whispered "Buen Camino" to my fellow pilgrims and reluctantly left the cozy rest spot behind. The path stretched ahead with more pastoral views—fields, farms, the occasional barking dog—before reaching San Justo and eventually the jarring sight of the stairs leading up to Astorga.

These zigzagged stairs made me think of the stairs leading up to a water slide at an amusement park. *The slide looks fun, but do I really want to climb all those stairs? Lazy river, anyone?*

I stared up at them. *Is this the only way into town?* I was honestly too tired to look for another route.

So up the stairs it was. One step at a time—the Camino's favorite joke, and its only promise.

*14*

# **Wild Thyme**

The layers of Astorga's history were in full view as I exited the staircase. Roman walls, medieval structures, Baroque facades, and modern buildings all competed for attention across the town's skyline, and I didn't know where to look first. There was something magnetic about how the town wore its age with pride, each era leaving its mark without erasing what came before. When a place doesn't just have a long history but actively holds onto it—even just pieces of it—it develops a character I want to get to know. It made me think of those newly developed neighborhoods back home that seem to spring up overnight. All clean lines and fresh paint, like movie sets waiting for stories to be inserted to give them life. In places like Astorga, history isn't something you visit in a museum—it's intertwined with the present, part of the very fabric of daily life.

I followed the signs to Albergue de Peregrinos Siervas de María, which became an albergue in 2006 after its conversion from a convent. I found Kathrine first, then located my room. Though I was sore from the day's walk, I didn't want to spend the afternoon resting. I changed into my sandals, and Kathrine and I stepped out to explore.

Our albergue was centrally located, which made getting around easy. We wandered through a few shops, eventually finding one selling eclectic clothing and jewelry. As we dug through dishes of stone rings, I noticed the music drifting through the shop. Indie acoustic songs that had served as a soundtrack to my high school and college years. Damien Rice, the Weepies, Peter Bradley Adams, basically any artist you might have heard in a coffee shop around 2007. Music that tastes like chai and feels like a warm sweater on a rainy day. It was unexpected and oddly comforting, this little pocket of familiarity in a medieval Spanish town.

We both purchased some jewelry, our fingers now adorned with new rings, and left the shop still humming with that warm nostalgia. The afternoon was slipping away, and we decided it was time to find dinner.

The small restaurant we chose had that worn in charm that made it feel like a local favorite. I checked the menu with the usual mix of hope and low expectations; gluten-free options can be nonexistent or astronomically priced. But there it was: a gluten-free section that didn't require a second mortgage. I ordered a burger, and Kathrine did the same. This was a welcome surprise. In fact, our entire meal for both of us cost about the same as a single fast food combo back home. The food was fresh, generous, and actually affordable. *Okay, I'm really loving Astorga.*

I honestly have no recollection of what came after dinner, which usually means I slept like a rock. What I do remember vividly was the following morning.

Kathrine and I stopped at a cafe for breakfast, and it was the perfect place to people watch. I mostly watched the woman serving coffee. In Spain, when cafes and stores have a lull, the staff doesn't scramble to look busy.

They take a break, pour themselves coffee, and actually enjoy it. Here was this woman, completely unhurried, savoring her espresso between customers like it were the most natural thing in the world.

I watched her serve someone their coffee, then calmly sit down with her own. *You go, girl.* There was no guilt, no glancing around to see if anyone noticed, no second-guessing. This was just her normal Thursday morning. She existed in a culture that had figured out something I was only beginning to understand: that constant motion isn't the same as productivity, and taking a breath doesn't make you lazy.

I think that's what bothered me most—not her, but myself. I'd always thought I was pretty easygoing and adaptable, but inside I carried this invisible timer, ticking away even when there was nothing to time. Years of retail work had probably drilled it into me. "If you're leaning, you're cleaning. Don't look idle. Keep moving, or customers will think you're lazy."

Spain was teaching me a different rhythm. One I kind of envied. And honestly? One I desperately needed to learn before my internal stopwatch gave me an ulcer.

Before we left town, we stopped at a chocolateria that had been around for over 100 years. The shop also sold souvenirs, and while I had brought a ball cap with me, I found myself drawn to a straw sun hat with a slight cowboy vibe. It was five euros—practically nothing. When I went up to the counter to purchase it and handed the shopkeeper my cash, she smiled and placed a small chocolate in my hand, just because. *Um, okay.*

I glanced through the glass case displaying other mouthwatering delicacies and pointed to something called Tarta de Santiago. The shopkeeper explained it was an almond cake, considered the unofficial dessert of the Camino de Santiago. I'd heard of it but hadn't tried it yet, apparently it was more popular along this stretch of the route. I looked closer at the powdered sugar-dusted cake, then noticed the small plaque next to it: Sin Gluten/Sin Lactosa. Gluten-free, lactose-free.

My heart took a little leap. *Okay, we need to leave because I'm pretty sure this town is flirting with me.*

From that point on, Tarta de Santiago would appear on almost every menu, and I would have something I could eat without worry for the rest of my Camino. It was such a small thing, but gosh, it felt like freedom.

Maybe it was the cake, my new hat, or the change of landscape as we left Astorga behind, but I felt giddy. My legs still ached, but I suddenly had a lot of energy. The pain was dull and persistent, but I could now tap into the energy I had lacked before. I felt lighter, like something inside me had finally exhaled.

And it was strange to realize this wasn't the first time I'd experienced this shift on the Camino. It kept happening: layers of restlessness and tension being chipped away, one after another. How many times could someone shed their old self so quickly? How many selves would one experience before arriving in Santiago?

As we left Astorga, the world around us began its transformation. The yellow dirt of the Meseta became intermingled with slate stone, and the wide pastoral fields gave way to wild thyme, broom, and scattered wildflowers. This area is called the Maragateria, the land of the mountain people, and the shift was undeniable. The air felt fresh—cooler, sharper. The horizon no longer stretched endlessly flat but rose and fell. We were being welcomed into mountain life, and I could feel my body responding to it, waking up in a new way.

It was this landscape that made me wish I had been a better science student. Vegetation and terrain surrounded me so captivating that I stopped every five minutes to touch something new; a fuzzy leaf, a delicate flower, the rough bark of a gnarled tree. I wanted to know the names of all the plants and flowers growing around us, to understand what I was walking through instead of just admiring it. I recognized thyme from its unmistakable smell and tucked a sprig into my hat, afraid of losing that sharp, herby scent as we made our way along the trail. This air, light, and wildness made me want to emulate Maria von Trapp and sing at the top of my lungs while twirling through the hills.

My knee pain had become an afterthought at best. We were ascending into the mountains, which very well could have kept my focus locked on aching joints and protesting muscles, but the scenery simply wouldn't allow for it. We entered Santa Catalina de Somoza, taking in the scenery: sage green brush with purple buds, a winding path, and distant mountains.

I had a new ache then. My face was sore from smiling.

Santa Catalina was one of my favorite towns on the Camino. It was a comfortably quiet place where you could hear your own thoughts without them competing with traffic or crowds. The stone buildings had cheerful colored doors and shutters—greens, blues, and sunny yellows—which seemed to announce that the life there was savored, not rushed. Our albergue had a patio painted emerald green and covered in potted plants spilling over their containers. The day was sunny and warm, so I changed into shorts and helped myself to a drink and a small dish of olives at an outdoor table, soaking in the day's light both externally and internally.

I pulled out my blue floral notebook, the one I'd been carrying since Leon, and tried to figure out a way to incorporate this mountain haven into my scribbled story. *Does it fit? Does it belong in this draft, or is it something else entirely?* I stared at the page, pen hovering. *Maybe I'll save it for another story. Maybe this place deserves its own space.*

But even as I considered it, I knew I'd write it down anyway, because some places refuse to be left behind.

I'm not prone to napping, but the fresh air and the sheer exhilaration of the day left me craving a bit of shut-eye. I rested for an hour or two. When I woke up, my good mood hadn't lessened; if anything, it had improved. The albergue restaurant offered a full paella menu. I was ready to celebrate with a proper meal, so I looked forward to trying their unique variations. Kathrine and I had purchased a bottle of wine to enjoy with our meal. We didn't finish it, so I carefully tucked it into the side pocket of my backpack, planning to share it with her the following night in Foncebadón.

My new straw hat had shifted something in me, I felt like a proper mountain woman now, like I belonged out here among the ridges and wildflowers. The following day, we saw a cowboy cantina with weathered wood and a hitching post. I had to pose for a picture. But we weren't in some romanticized version of America; we were in Spanish cowboy country, the Maragato heartland. Kathrine and I passed countless pastures dotted with mules, cows, and horses, their bells clanking softly as they grazed against the backdrop of rolling mountains.

The ascent was becoming steeper with each kilometer, but the scenery continued to demand our attention, refusing to let us focus too much on our burning calves or labored breathing. In Rabanal del Camino, I found a moment of peace at the Iglesia de la Asunción. This 12th century church still conducts services.

I lit a candle and sat on one of the weathered wooden pews, just letting the stillness settle around me. The stone walls held a coolness that felt ancient, reverent. *How many pilgrims have sat here? How many prayers have been whispered into this same silence?* I closed my eyes and let the quiet seep in, aware that I was hesitant to leave but knowing I needed to keep moving. The mountains were drawing me in, stirring something in me I had no name for—something restless and alive and deeply, unexpectedly joyful.

When I finally stepped back outside, the light felt brighter, sharper. Kathrine was waiting, and we continued our climb together.

Before walking into Foncebadón, we stopped at some empty picnic tables perched on the hillside. We sat in silence for a moment, peering out at the tree-lined peaks stretching around us in every direction. The wind moved through the trees with a sound like breathing. I pulled out my phone and played "Captivated" by Shawn McDonald, letting the gentle melody drift between us. The words poured over us like a benediction, settling into the ground that seemed to hum and sing along. *This is it*, I thought. *This is what I came here for.* Not just the walking, not just the destination, but these moments when everything feels sacred, and the world opens itself up to you without asking for anything in return.

*15*

# What You Carry

Foncebadón is the last stop before Cruz de Ferro, and it definitely feels like it. There's anticipation in the air, a quiet intensity among the pilgrims gathered there. You can sense it—the knowledge that you're only a couple of kilometers away from a place that has held emotional and spiritual weight for centuries, a site that has drawn pilgrims to lay down their burdens.

People consider Cruz de Ferro the oldest marker on the Camino, older than many churches and monasteries along the route. It's a monument to surrendered burdens, a place where pilgrims have carried stones, physical representations of grief, regret, hope, shame, or simply the weight of life, and left them at the base of a towering iron cross.

And now I was almost there.

After getting settled in our albergue and after a warm dinner of mushroom and bean soup, Kathrine and I found ourselves another picnic table to sit and enjoy the rest of our wine. The setting sun gave the mountain range a purple hue, and it only added to the feeling that we were somewhere special.

Everyone in our room had the same plan: get there at sunrise. Someone set an alarm for us all to wake at the same time — a collective pilgrimage within the pilgrimage. For those of us who had never been there before, the more seasoned pilgrims shaped our expectations—as was true for so much of the Camino. They spoke of it as a place of enormous significance, a place that would help heal us of our burdens, where something intangible but undeniable might shift inside you.

I had been ruminating on the motif of pain and peace for most of my pilgrimage, and I had the sense that Cruz de Ferro was a place that recognized that strange marriage—that you could hold both at once, that maybe you were supposed to.

Cruz de Ferro sits at one of the tallest points in Spain, Monte Irago, and hosts a shrine made entirely of stones left by pilgrims. You can pick up your stone at any point along the Camino, or bring one from home— something small enough to carry but heavy enough to mean something. Laying it down at the base of the towering iron cross symbolizes the laying down of your burdens at the foot of the cross, a physical act of release that somehow makes the internal work feel more real.

Leaving the albergue, we turned on our headlamps and started towards the tree-lined path, everyone quiet. The faint beams of light cut through the predawn darkness, illuminating the narrow trail ahead and the gnarled roots snaking across the ground.

Not that I was expecting lots of chatter, it was early, after all, but this silence en route to the peak did nothing but put my expectations into overdrive. *Will I really be moved by a pile of pebbles? What if I walk right past it and miss it?* The path began to climb more steeply, and the trees thinned. Through the gaps, I could see the sky beginning to lighten at the edges, a soft blue bleeding into deep purple and orange.

When we finally reached the site and the iron cross came into view—tall and stark against the awakening sky, surrounded by its massive cairn of stones—I remember my thoughts racing: *What am I feeling, what am I feeling, what am I feeling?*

*Oh, shut up, Amy! Just stop trying to analyze everything and just BE HERE.*

*I think I'm hungry.*

*Will I cry when I lay my stone down? What am I supposed to feel?*

*Shut up!*

*Are my eyes welling up or do I need to sneeze?*

*Ugh.*

There were people who just tossed their stones onto the pile, quick and matter-of-fact, and others who covered them in tears before gently laying them down, their shoulders shaking with the weight of what they were releasing.

We were all there for different reasons. Some carried heavier burdens than others—grief that had names and faces, regrets that had followed them for years, fears they couldn't speak aloud. Yet, peace swept over that peak each time a new stone was laid, no matter its weight. The air felt sacred, hushed, like the mountain itself was holding space for us.

I had picked up my stone just outside of St. Jean Pied-de-Port, at the very beginning of my journey. On a torn-out page from my journal, I had written a prayer—words I'd been carrying in my heart long before I set foot on the Camino—and fastened it to the rock with a hair tie. Now, standing at the base of the iron cross with the sun just breaking over the horizon, I carefully stepped onto the stone pile and made my way toward the center. I ran my fingers over my stone one last time, tracing its rough edges, and whispered the prayer I had wrapped around it. Then, gently, I laid it down among the thousands of others and stepped back, giving the pilgrims behind me the space they needed for their own offerings.

There are picnic tables scattered all around Cruz de Ferro, and a secluded path that leads down to a water fountain tucked into the hillside. And this is where my expectations were wiped away, not at the cross itself, but here, at this quiet fountain overlooking the treetops.

It was this spot that moved me beyond the laying down of my stone. Something about the stillness, the way the light filtered through the branches, the sound of water trickling into the stone basin, it all felt like an invitation. *Stay here. Be still. Listen.*

It is often this spot I return to now in my quiet time. In moments when I'm trying to listen for God's voice, when the noise of life feels too loud, I close my eyes and sit on that ledge again, water bottle in hand, sunrise breaking over the trees. And He meets me there, just as He did that morning.

Every single time.

As I went to join Kathrine at our picnic table, I felt as though another set of boots was walking alongside my own. Though I had believed that Jesus was with me from the beginning of this journey, it was that morning that made me understand He wasn't just along for the ride; something had shifted. We would interact differently now. *He's here. Really here.*

Kathrine and I ate our packed breakfast quietly as we watched pilgrims approach the sacred peak. I found myself reaching over to the space next to me on the bench, half expecting to feel a hand cover my own. It sounds strange to say it, but I could sense a presence there; steady, warm, unmistakable.

I don't know how to really explain it other than this: the "thin place" I had been searching for had found its way to me, *in* me. The secluded mountainside fountain had become my secret place, and it was a holy warmth that settled itself in my bones, deeper than any cold could reach. I didn't want to ask God for anything except for the moment to last—to stretch and hold, to root itself so firmly in my memory that I could return to it whenever I needed to remember what peace felt like.

In all my years as a believer in Christ, I think this was the first time I truly knew what it meant to "delight yourself in the Lord" (Psalm 37:4). Not as a concept or a verse to memorize, but as a lived reality—joy without effort, presence without striving.

I thanked Him for the Camino. I thanked Him for the injuries that had slowed me down enough to notice. I thanked Him for the previous two years of stress and anxiety that had driven me here. If all of it—the pain, the uncertainty, the unraveling—had brought me to this place, to this moment, then I was grateful. Deeply, achingly grateful.

And it was that gratitude that followed me the rest of the day, settling into my stride like yet another companion. It helped that the scenery was jaw-droppingly beautiful. The ruggedness of the trail—rocky, uneven, demanding—mixed with the wild awakening of the morning was intoxicating. The mountains rolled out before us in waves of green and gray, and there were plants I couldn't name but knew I'd miss when I left.

My knee was sore, and I still had blisters, but I was humming. I was walking with Jesus, and for the first time in a long time, it didn't feel like a metaphor or a pleasant idea. It felt real.

My thoughts were shifting from internal analysis to conversations with Him.

*Look over there! You made that?*

A cluster of purple flowers spills down a hillside like paint.

*Did you make it just for me? Kind of feels like you did.*

And maybe that's silly; maybe it's childish to think the Creator of the universe would arrange wildflowers for one tired pilgrim on a Spanish mountain. But at that moment, it didn't feel silly at all.

We were descending into the valley and had planned on stopping at El Acebo. This was one of our shortest walking days, but after an early and emotional morning at Cruz de Ferro, it was enough. My body was ready to be done, and my heart needed time to process everything that had happened on that mountain.

The sharp decline was a combination of loose gravel and jagged rock, and though my eyes were constantly tempted to drink in the sweeping views of the valley below, I needed to watch my step. One wrong move and I'd be sliding down on my backside.

*Lord, I am so grateful for everything You have done for me so far on this pilgrimage. I would be even more grateful to not do a face plant right now. Please and thank you. Amen.*

I made it into the village without falling and stopped at the first cafe I saw. Coffee hadn't touched my lips yet, and I didn't care if my albergue was literally next door—I was stopping here first. Though I was still buzzing spiritually from the morning's encounter, I was ready for a caffeine buzz too. And why rush inside when the sun was still up? After what I'd experienced, I wanted to stay out here a little longer, let the warmth soak into my skin like a benediction and the light stretch the day out, as if I could hold on to this feeling just a bit more.

El Acebo overlooks the valley below, and the village itself is a picture of quintessential medieval mountain living: stone buildings with slate roofs, narrow cobbled streets, wooden balconies overflowing with flowers. It all felt perfectly suited to this seemingly unspoiled region, like it had grown out of the mountainside rather than been built upon it. I claimed a table on the patio, ordered an Americano, and let myself just be—grateful, tired, and completely at peace.

Kathrine joined me after a while, and after finishing another coffee or two, we begrudgingly left the cafe and its view, heading down the narrow stone street to our albergue.

But when we arrived, we discovered it had a huge patio with even more panoramic views of the valley below. The mountains stretched out in layers of blue and green, fading into the hazy distance, and the late afternoon light painted everything golden. A few other pilgrims were across the patio, reading or writing in journals, and I felt the same quiet contentment settling into my chest.

Kathrine and I exchanged knowing and contented smiles as we walked along the patio's edge side by side. We didn't need to say it out loud—we both knew. This was a good day. Maybe the best day.

We stood there in comfortable silence, occasionally pointing out something in the distance or sharing a quiet observation, but mostly just letting the moment be what it was. The sun began its slow descent, and I realized I didn't want this day to end—not because I knew the next day was literally all downhill, but because something had shifted in me, and I wasn't ready to let the evening carry it away just yet.

*Thank you for today.*

# 16

# **Antsy Pants**

I recently read a story about St. Francis of Assisi that made me smile. He was walking down a street in the dead of winter and saw a bare, withered almond tree. Being the quirky saint that he was, Francis walked up to the tree and said, "Sister almond tree! Speak to me of God!" And the bare tree burst into bloom.

These were the words I believe some pilgrim saint spoke to the mountains in León just before I stepped foot onto them. *Speak to me of God.* And they did. They spoke in the language of beauty and wildness, and light. Air is vital for survival, but there was something about the air in this place that went beyond necessity—it was invigorating, alive, like breathing in grace itself. It wasn't just the air. Sunlight completely saturated everything.

I kind of get why some cultures worship the sun. The Egyptians called it Ra; the Greeks, Helios. The Celts had Lugh; the Japanese had Amaterasu; the Hindus, Surya. Apollo, Inti, Mitra, Freyr, Shamash—name a culture, and they probably had a sun deity. When St. Francis asked that almond tree to speak to him of God, he wasn't worshipping the tree—he was recognizing it as part of God's chorus. A fellow creature giving glory. I think that's what those ancient sun worshippers were responding to. They felt the warmth on their skin, watched it coax life from the ground, experienced how it lifted their spirits on dark days—and they knew, deep in their bones, that something about this was sacred. The sun is an incredibly generous gift. It warms, it feeds, it sustains, it affects our very moods. "The heavens declare the glory of God, and the sky above proclaims his handiwork" (Psalm 19:1). The sun has been faithfully doing its job of declaring since day four of creation, and honestly? It's really, really good at it. I found myself tilting my face toward it constantly, even though I was already getting plenty of sun exposure on the trail. Some gifts are just too good not to soak up.

The sunshine that woke the greenery around us and helped us ease our aching bones into the rhythm of walking fueled the days ascending and descending the mountains. Songs of worship were readily on my lips, hummed and sung softly as each step brought me further into the wild landscape of the Montes de León.

Those days especially, I had faces of friends and family coming to mind frequently as I got to behold a new scenic view at every turn. *Gosh, I wish so-and-so could see this.* Or, *I know that so-and-so would LOVE this.* I had moments of guilt that I was given this trail and so many others were missing out, that I got to be here and they didn't.

And I still felt the boots beside me. The glory-filled time by the fountain the day before hadn't faded—it was still going strong, woven into every step, every breath, every moment of wonder. *Walking with Jesus.* The phrase had always felt a little abstract to me before, something people said in church without really thinking about what it meant. But out here, on this trail, it was becoming literal in a way I'd never experienced.

And maybe that's because walking itself had always been sacred to me—I just hadn't realized it until now. I have always been a walker. I knew the pavement around my hometown better than the back of my hand. If it weren't for joggers, bikers, rollerbladers, children, and dogs, I could walk that trail safely with my eyes closed. Sure, it was only a mile long, but I knew it well.

The Traverse City Civic Center path was where I did all of my deep thinking. I listened to my favorite CDs, and I prayed—a lot. I walked barefoot, in sandals, in worn shoes patched with duct tape, rarely in sensible footwear. I would do a few laps around and walk back home. That was my place to let my heart and mind work things out to the rhythm of my steps.

In college, I walked from campus through the surrounding neighborhoods to the closest Tim Hortons, where I'd remember I was broke and it would end up being just a thinking walk, not a coffee-drinking walk. Studying in the U.K. was a walker's dream. Not only was it my primary mode of transportation, but in Oxford, I wasn't just walking to class—I was walking in the steps of my literary heroes, tracing paths that C.S. Lewis and J.R.R. Tolkien had walked decades before.

Finally, after moving to west Michigan, I found myself walking the neighborhood, uninspired. I had to drive to the closest park, and after a time, I mostly walked at my retail jobs—pacing the aisles, restocking shelves, always moving but never really going anywhere. I don't think I ever really gave it much thought until I started working on this book. Walking has been sacred to me for most of my life.

That rhythm I'd found in my hometown walks, in Oxford's ancient streets—it was here too, carrying me down from El Acebo with renewed purpose. It was a steep descent, leaving El Acebo and I absolutely loved it! My knee and foot were in pain, but the trail was glorious and the weather sublime! We walked through

Molinaseca, a very pretty town nestled in the mountains. Much like Hospital de Orbigo, it looked locked in the 12th century. We stopped at a small shop and stocked up on some snacks before continuing on to Ponferrada.

Then it was hot and not so attractive going towards Ponferrada, but once we arrived, it was a beautiful city! A large medieval fortress at its center, cafes all around—gorgeous. We were hot and tired, but we made it to our hotel, cleaned up, and Kathrine treated us to a taxi back into town—so worth it. We visited the Templar castle, got some snacks and drinks. I had a terribly upset stomach, but Kathrine was patient with me as we made it back to our hotel. Kathrine went to the hotel restaurant, and I stayed in the room while watching church online and eating rice cakes and banana chips.

Our rest day in Ponferrada fell on Labour Day in Spain, which meant most things were closed. The hotel was peaceful and restful, but even with my upset stomach the night before, I couldn't shake the restlessness. I wanted to be back in the mountains, back in the thick of other pilgrims and the rhythm of the trail. I felt more alive and inspired on the road, especially in this region. After those days of walking with Jesus so tangibly by my side, I was itching to move, to see what would happen next, to find out what else He wanted to show me out there.

I have always been a fast walker. I've lost count of the number of times I've heard someone in my family yell, "Amy! You have to wait for everyone! Slow down!" And I would usually respond with something like, "I can't help it! This is my natural pace!" Considering how easily others overtook me on the Camino trail, I'm now convinced I come from a family of sloths. (Just kidding, guys!)

That morning, I was walking fast around the nearly empty streets of Ponferrada, restless and ready. Alba was right that this city was beautiful—the fortress, the cafes, the medieval charm—but I wanted to get back to the mountain trail. Not that I was in a rush to finish the Camino, but I was actually getting antsy. I was looking for backpacks lining the outer walls of the cafes and listened for the clicking of walking sticks.

*What am I really itching for?* I wondered as Kathrine and I finally shouldered our packs and headed out of the city the next day.

The day we left Ponferrada definitely satiated my thirst to get a move on. After a short bus ride out of town, we had twenty-four kilometers ahead of us to reach La Faba, and even though much of it was along the highway—not exactly inspiring—I found it went by surprisingly quickly. We passed through some residential and suburban neighborhoods that felt oddly out of place after days in the mountains, before eventually returning to more forested areas and winding paths that felt like coming home.

Kathrine and I walked separately for most of the day, our respective injuries forcing us into different paces. When I reached the small town of La Portela de Valcarce, I ducked into the Iglesia de San Juan Bautista, a tiny church that I had all to myself for a few precious moments of stillness. I sat in a pew, caught my breath, and let the quiet settle around me like a blanket.

My knee was tight, but I was feeling good—strong, even—until I reached the climb into La Faba. It wasn't very long objectively speaking, but it felt long. It was a winding forest trail beautifully canopied by twisting trees, but STEEP. I was drenched in sweat and ready to collapse when I wheezily stumbled into town. Naturally, I found Kathrine already at the albergue cafe, casually sipping a beer like she hadn't just walked twenty-four kilometers. Her blisters had burst earlier in the day, and she'd had to take a taxi for the last six kilometers. She looked far too relaxed for someone whose feet had recently staged a mutiny. It helped that the outdoor tables overlooked the stunning scenery I had just clambered through.

Our host was a very fun, sweet guy named Tito, who had only just opened this albergue. He was generous with food and homemade schnapps—very generous with the schnapps, actually—and his enthusiasm for hosting pilgrims was contagious. Our room was small and had only a couple of bunks, but a brightly colored fleece blanket covered each bed, giving the space a cozy, welcoming feel. I showered off the day's sweat and grime, then took some time to write in both my journal and story notebook. My walking conversations with Jesus were taking up more and more space in my journal those days, and I still had moments when my story ideas had room to develop and share the trail with us, weaving themselves into the rhythm of my steps.

Before calling it a night, I joined some of the other pilgrims downstairs. That's when I got to have a nice, long chat with an Irish pilgrim who had been on the Camino since the end of February. *February!* He was planning on heading to America next, just to keep the adventure going. As much as I loved the Camino, I couldn't fathom being out here for that long. I was already missing my family and friends, actually feeling the pull of home.

The bittersweet truth was settling in: the ending here would be the beginning of a new chapter back home, and I wasn't sure I was ready for either. As I climbed into my bunk that night, I thought about that Irish pilgrim downstairs, still planning his next adventure. Meanwhile, I was already homesick. *Some wanderer I turned out to be.*

But maybe that was okay. Maybe walking with Jesus didn't mean I had to pick one or the other—the restless urge to keep moving or the pull toward home. He was in both. In the itchy feet that got me here and the longing that would eventually carry me back.

I pulled Tito's bright fleece blanket up to my chin, still feeling those boots beside me, and let myself drift off. *Tomorrow, more mountains. But tonight, I can admit that I miss my people.*

*17*

# Go the Distance

I needed Disney music for my walk to Triacastela. We started the day with a steady climb to O Cebreiro, and when we reached the peak, we stood above the clouds. Literally above them. Beautiful cotton-like clouds covered the valley below, and the silhouettes of mountains rose through the mist, appearing to beg to come closer. It was the kind of view that makes you stop walking just to stare, the kind that makes you understand why people have been making pilgrimages to this place for over a thousand years.

Galicia gave a very good first impression. Her aged stone buildings—some dating back to the 9th century—sat nestled into the landscape. The trees were stunning, with twisted trunks and canopies that filtered the light into something almost magical. Oak and chestnut forests stretched on for kilometers, their branches creating natural cathedrals overhead. The horizon rolled on and on in waves of green.

*This is amazing. I'm in Middle Earth again!*

Small villages appeared along the path like they were in no rush to modernize; stone houses with slate roofs, tiny churches with wooden doors worn smooth by centuries of hands, gardens where old women tended vegetables the way their grandmothers probably had. Everything felt slower here. Deliberate. Like Galicia knew it had something worth preserving and wasn't about to let the modern world rush it along.

My knee, however, was less than impressed.

I cannot overstate how gorgeous the day was, but my stupid knee wasn't having it. The descent from O Cebreiro was brutal—all downhill, all pressure, all pain. My thoughts were intermingled with prayers as they had been for days, but these prayers had a more desperate tone to them.

*Puhleeeeaaasssseee, Lord. TAKE THE KNEE.*
*I don't care how you do it!*
*Heal it. Disintegrate it. Chop it clean off.*
*I. DON'T. CARE.*

This is what hundreds of kilometers will do to your prayer life—it gets very honest, very quickly. A little less "Thy will be done" and more "PLEASE MAKE IT STOP." I'd like to say I was praying with faith and patience, but mostly I was just limping and complaining to God about it. Which is also prayer. Not the kind they teach you in Sunday school, but prayer nonetheless.

I stopped for lunch at a small cafe and ordered a salad, which seemed like a safe choice until I started eating it. There were a few mystery ingredients that my stomach immediately rejected. *What else is new?*

Kathrine and I weren't walking together that day: her blisters, my knee, different paces, different needs. For the most part, the trail was pretty clear, which meant I could walk without having to think too hard about where I was going.

So I did what any reasonable person would do when they're in pain, slightly nauseous, and walking through one of the most beautiful landscapes in Europe: I plugged in my headphones and belted out "Hakuna Matata" at the top of my lungs.

Look, I'm not proud of it. But also, I'm not *not* proud of it.

There's something about Disney music that hits differently when you're suffering. Maybe it's the nostalgia, or the relentless optimism, or that every song is basically telling you that everything's going to be okay, even when your knee feels like it's made of broken glass and your stomach is making whale sounds.

I moved through the entire *Lion King* soundtrack, then switched to *Tarzan* and *Mulan*. By the time I reached *Frozen*, I'd found my rhythm again. The pain didn't disappear miraculously; somehow, it just felt more manageable. More bearable.

It was like the music gave my brain something else to focus on besides the screaming from my joints. Each song became a milestone—*Just make it through "I'll Make a Man Out of You," then you can assess. Just finish "Let It Go," then decide if you need to stop.* The kilometers started passing in three-minute increments instead of endless stretches of suffering. Small goals. Achievable distances. One Disney song at a time.

I passed a few other pilgrims on the trail, and I like to think they appreciated my impromptu concert. (They probably didn't. But I was too focused on not falling to care). *I can go the distance...*

The thing about pilgrimage is that it strips away all your pretenses. You can't maintain a dignified, spiritual persona when your body is falling apart and you're eating mystery salad and singing Disney songs to yourself like a maniac. You just become... yourself. The limping, slightly ridiculous version of yourself who needs Timon and Pumbaa to get through the day.

By the time I finally stumbled into Triacastela, I was exhausted, in pain, and probably smelled terrible. But I'd made it. Twenty-seven kilometers, one bad knee, one worse salad, and an entire Disney playlist later—I'd made it.

The town sat nestled in a valley, its name meaning "three castles," though I only spotted remnants of old fortifications on the surrounding hills. Stone houses lined narrow streets, and the evening light made everything glow golden. The albergue had a large deck with a spectacular view, which felt like a reward for surviving the day's descent. I claimed a spot out there immediately. Even after spending the entire day walking through such beautiful scenery, and singing my way through the Disney catalog like a maniac, I didn't want to miss a thing. My knee might have been staging a rebellion, but my eyes were still working just fine. I sat there nursing a drink and watching the valley settle into evening, feeling utterly exhausted and completely content at the same time.

The next stage of the trail felt like the calm before the storm. We'd been told to expect a more crowded trail once we reached Sarria, just a few kilometers ahead, but until then, Galicia continued to work its magic. The forests grew denser, more enchanted. I half expected to see hobbits around every corner. The path wound through ancient woodland where moss covered everything and streams trickled over rocks that had probably been there since before Spain was Spain.

Celtic art appeared—stone markers carved with spirals and knots, tiny chapels barely bigger than closets where candles flickered in the dim light. Some villages we passed through looked like they'd opted out of the last few centuries entirely. No rush. No urgency. Just people living in rhythm with the land, the way they always had.

Sarria. The town bustled with outdoor gear shops displaying walking poles and moisture-wicking shirts stamped with scallop shell symbols. Fresh pilgrims everywhere, comparing blister remedies they hadn't needed yet, taking selfies with their pristine boots.

Between Sarria and Portomarín, the landscape opened up into rolling green hills and oak forests. Beauty that would've stolen my breath if I wasn't too busy trying to navigate around tour groups. We'd entered "the 100K zone"—where people who only had time to walk the final 100 kilometers joined the Camino. People who'd been walking for weeks suddenly shared the trail with fresh-faced walkers who still had the tags on their hiking boots. The quiet rhythm we'd settled into had shifted into something louder, more chaotic.

I tried not to be annoyed. *They're here for the same reasons you are. Be nice.* But there was something jarring about it—the sudden shift from solitude to crowds, from contemplation to conversation, from "I'm having a spiritual experience" to "Excuse me, can you take our photo?"

The trail itself became more managed here, with clearer markers and more facilities. The wildness of the earlier stages gave way to something more curated. Which had its benefits—better bathrooms, more cafes, actual places to buy food that wouldn't send your stomach into rebellion. But it also felt like we were leaving something behind. That raw, unfiltered version of the Camino where it was just you and the path and whatever God wanted to say to you along the way.

By the time we reached Portomarín, I'd walked through enough hills and forests to last a lifetime. The town sat above a reservoir—they'd flooded the original village in the 1960s and moved everything to higher ground, stone by stone. The church of San Nicolás had been disassembled and rebuilt, which felt oddly fitting for a pilgrimage route. Everything old is new again. Everything broken gets reassembled.

I slept like the dead that afternoon—a deep two-hour nap that left me groggy when I woke. I dragged myself up just in time for someone to invite us to join some other pilgrims for drinks. We sat at an outdoor table as dusk settled in, watching wave after wave of new arrivals finding their way through town. Fresh faces, clean clothes, unblistered feet. That's when one of our companions—an Irish guy named Philip—asked if we'd come across anyone walking the Camino for religious reasons. Kathrine pointed at me. I hesitantly raised my hand. Philip had complicated feelings about the Catholic Church and asked me about my thoughts on it and how it had brought me here. To his surprise, I told him I wasn't Catholic—I just wanted to come and thought it would help grow my faith. That was it. I wish I had given a more eloquent answer, but the word "religious" made me pause. I could be completely uninhibited about "Hakuna Matata" but tongue-tied about Jesus.

After we said our goodnights, I went straight back to bed and slept through until morning, exhausted. Philip's question stayed with me.

The next day, as the trail wound through more villages, past fields and farms and the occasional chapel tucked into the hillside, I kept turning his words over in my mind. *Did I come for religious reasons?* The honest answer was complicated. I'd spent years trying to share my faith without sounding like the judgmental kid I used to be — the one who had all the answers and none of the grace. But here I was, walking an ancient pilgrimage route that most people in the modern world find completely foreign. Too impractical. Too slow. Too medieval. We're too busy, too rational, too convinced that there are more efficient ways to find God.

And yet.

I thought about all the reasonable off-ramps I'd passed on the way to this trail. The slow intellectual pressure — the suggestion that faith, on its own, is somehow insufficient, that it needs updating or qualifying or a more sophisticated framework bolted onto the side. Bearing the weight of the past few years: the pandemic, the political clamor, and the distinct heartache of watching the hope for something greater slowly diminish. The personal losses, the kind that don't make the news but leave a mark that doesn't fully lift. Each one had been a reasonable exit. Each one asked, not unkindly, whether I was really sure about this.

I kept choosing to stay. Not because the doubts weren't real, or because I had answers that neatly resolved them. Just because every time I looked honestly at the alternatives, nothing else held.

There's a moment in John's gospel that I kept coming back to on the trail. The crowds are drifting away from Jesus — put off by the cost of following, unwilling to go where this was heading. He turns to His closest friends and asks quietly if they're leaving too. And Peter, with the honest exhaustion of someone who has already looked at every other option, answers: "Lord, to whom shall we go?" (John 6:68)

That's it. That's the whole thing. Not a dramatic moment of clarity. Not a feeling chased until it made sense. Just a person who had looked at every door and found that only one of them led somewhere real. Because by the time you're on day thirty-something, knee held together with willpower and ibuprofen, singing Disney songs just to keep moving — you're not performing faith anymore. You're just telling the truth about what you actually have left.

What I had left was Him. And it turned out that was enough.

The trail continued winding through more villages, past fields, and the occasional chapel tucked into a hillside. I kept running into reminders of what I'd been missing. People praying the rosary as they walked, the repetition almost musical — devotion made audible. Something both foreign and familiar, a rhythm of faith that looked different from mine but came from the same place. Faith with feet. Traditions with weight.

It was just a few days to Santiago now. I came looking for clarity, healing, a new lease on life. But as the kilometers passed, those personal reasons deepened into something richer. I heard his whispers in the wind and felt His hand on my shoulder when I felt out of place. Being surrounded by Catholics praying rosaries, people seeking their own spiritual paths, people with complicated faith histories — it helped me fall back in love with being a Christian. Not the version I'd sometimes performed in my youth, concerned with being right and having answers. But the version where Jesus actually feels like good news. He is there for all of it. Where you can pray desperate prayers and sing silly songs and talk honestly about your doubts, and all of it counts as sacred.

Faith that hurts and hopes.

Pain and joy aren't opposites — sometimes they're just two sides of the same stubborn faith. That version of myself — undignified, hurting, but somehow still singing — felt more free than anything I'd been in a long time. The God who meets you in desperate knee prayers on mountain descents and Disney songs when your body is falling apart. The God who shows up in conversations with strangers on dusty trails, in ancient stone churches and albergues, in rosary beads and the quiet moments when you realize you're not walking alone. And you never were.

*18*

# A Kiss From Fernando

The trail was overrun. Pilgrims as far as the eye could see. I found myself speed walking along the road to get around the clusters of students that insisted on walking arm-in-arm, taking up the entire path like some kind of teenage human chain.

I was walking faster than I had in weeks, and it was purely for the sake of personal space. I realized the irony of hiking hundreds of kilometers on a pilgrimage route only to end up practically jogging away from other pilgrims.

That's when I saw signs for the Castro de Castromaior detour and decided to follow it. The turnoff was easy to miss—just a small wooden sign pointing up a narrower path. It wasn't a far detour, maybe just a few minutes off the main route, but it was enough to get me some breathing room.

The path climbed slightly, winding through scrubby bushes and wildflowers, and then suddenly opened up. I arrived at the archaeological site and stopped. The place was completely empty. *I have an Iron Age excavation all to myself!*

I meandered through the ruins, trying to make sense of the layout. The outer defensive walls formed a rough circle, their stones still stacked in places, tumbled in others. Soft green moss covered some walls, looking bright against the gray rock.

In the center, I could make out the foundations of what must have been buildings—circles within circles, rooms within rooms. I stepped carefully over the low walls, imagining where doorways might have been, where families might have gathered.

From the highest point of the outer mounds, the entire landscape spread out before me. Rolling hills of green, stitched together with stone walls and dotted with yellow and purple wildflowers. And there, cutting through the valley below, was the Camino trail. I could see the pilgrims—tiny figures moving in clusters and alone, steadily making their way forward. I watched them for a few moments, wondering if any of them knew how close they were to a 2,000-year-old fortress.

I couldn't believe I didn't need to buy a ticket for this experience. No gate, no fee, no staff. Just this ancient place, open and waiting for whoever was curious enough to take the detour.

I stayed up there for a little while longer, finally settling on a sun-warmed stone. There, the history felt alive, not in a spooky way, but in the way old places feel when people have loved, used, and remembered them. I sat and smiled. All by myself. It was perfect.

After a few minutes, some more people found their way to the ruins, and I took my leave. Another wave of students was on my heels on the trail, so I picked up the pace again. (Former youth leader or not, there's only so much patience a person can muster.) Once I made it to Palas de Rei, I connected with Kathrine and found out that we would stay in the same albergue as the teens. *Joy.*

But as luck would have it, we had a smaller, separated room that we would share with some older, friendly Chinese pilgrims. Kathrine and I walked into our room to find the students were only a muffled sound in the distance.

*At last! Some quiet!* Our roommates weren't around, but there was another presence in the room that was impossible to ignore: their food. Our fellow travelers had left a bowl of hard-boiled eggs to just sit in the room. Just sitting there. On the table. In the warm room.

It wasn't yet suppertime, so the smell, while unpleasant, wasn't too strong. We figured it would go away once the eggs were consumed. We discovered too late that those eggs were being saved for breakfast the next morning. Breakfast. The. Next. Morning.

The windows in our room had to be closed to muffle the sound of the church bells next door—those bells that rang every single hour, all night long. With the windows shut, the eggs began to percolate and infuse everything within a ten-foot radius with their scent. I smelled eggs in my hair! It didn't matter how far I buried my head beneath my sleeping bag; the smell followed me there.

As you might imagine, the next day was our earliest start. After very little sleep, I woke up to Kathrine standing over me with a stern face. "Get up, we're leaving." I checked my watch. 5:30 a.m. We were out of there before those eggs could assault us one more time.

Gosh, was I grateful for the breeze that day. But aside from the aftermath of breathing egg-air all night, I felt like I really had to choose to enjoy this day. It wasn't coming naturally. The beauty of the mountains helped, but there, amidst the bed race, the heat, the eggs—the cursed, cursed eggs—I was nearly crawling out of my skin.

Kathrine and I had walked separately a few times in those days. Not that we didn't want to be around each other—we'd been through too much together for that—but we were trying to listen to our bodies and the pain they were expressing. My legs were screaming different things than hers. We always stayed at the same place, though. We were booking things ahead, trying to avoid the afternoon scramble.

Even when we walked separately, we had a system. Every few kilometers, one of us would slow down at a cafe or rest stop until the other caught up. We'd exchange a look—*You good?*—maybe grab a quick coffee, and then continue on. We didn't need to walk side-by-side to walk together. After everything we'd been through, I knew exactly where she'd be at the end of the day.

One night we met up with some of our friends at their albergue for dinner. The albergue was run by a man named Fernando and his wife. We sat at an outdoor table, and Fernando gave us the royal treatment. I've spoken often about the generosity of the Camino, and this was a very special reminder of that.

He gave each guest one hundred percent of his attention. Fernando laid each plate with care and accompanied it with a hearty smile. He moved between tables, checking on everyone, making sure we had everything we needed. His eyes crinkled when he smiled, which was basically always.

Even though Kathrine and I were staying at the albergue next door—we'd already paid, already dropped our packs—he treated us as if we were his granddaughters. He seemed genuinely touched that we would eat at his establishment. He gave us all hugs as we finished our meal, holding on just a moment longer than necessary. Kathrine and I walked back to our albergue, wishing we would have stayed with Fernando instead.

The next morning I woke up before Kathrine and got a text from our friends asking if I wanted to join them at their albergue for breakfast.

Fernando, with a huge smile on his face, gave me the biggest piece of cake I've ever seen. I wasn't about to tell him I wasn't supposed to eat gluten. I felt he had put so much love into that breakfast that the natural effect gluten had on me would be void.

His albergue was a quiet one, filled with books and memorabilia from a life before the Camino. This wasn't just an albergue; it was a home, opened up to sweaty strangers with blisters.

He told us that he and his wife had opened the albergue three years before. And then, of course, the pandemic hit. His eyes grew distant when he mentioned it. Two years of empty tables. Two years of waiting for the pilgrims to return.

There were so many times on the Camino that I completely forgot COVID existed. I was so caught up in the journey's magic—the walking, the simplicity, the daily rhythm of putting one foot in front of the other. But standing in front of me was a man who had borne the brunt of it, and it was heartbreaking.

My friends and I were trying to translate words of encouragement and thanks as best we could, fumbling between English, Spanish, and enthusiastic hand gestures. We weren't about to let the kindness he had shown us go unnoticed. He had tears in his eyes and hugged each of us as we made our way out the door.

He held onto my shoulders and planted a loving, grandfatherly kiss on my cheek. The tenderness of it caught me completely off guard. I wanted to cry. So I kissed him back.

My friends and I left the albergue heading toward the square. We turned around after we crossed the street, and Fernando was still waving to us from the door. We waved back. He kept waving. We walked further and turned again. Still waving. The man was committed to his goodbyes.

Fernando emulated kindness and selflessness. He was generous with the little he had, but his warm, sweet nature left a mark on me and my friends. That day didn't feel as hot and crowded because of it. Fernando came with me as I walked.

It's not abnormal to greet one another with kisses on the cheek, especially in Europe. I knew this. But I felt Fernando's kiss on my cheek for the rest of the day. My mind kept going back to him waving goodbye, standing in that doorway. *Why can't I think of anything else? Why does this feel so significant?*

**The Camino is releasing you.**

I stopped in my tracks. That thought did not come from me. I checked in with the boots next to mine. It was Jesus. *What do you mean?*

**Fernando was the Camino, saying goodbye.**

I stepped over to the side of the trail and let a few pilgrims pass me as I let that settle in. I had been feeling ready to get to Santiago—tired, eager for a proper shower, ready for a bed that didn't screech every time I rolled over. But at that moment, I seriously considered turning around and heading back to Saint Jean Pied-de-Port. Back to the beginning. Back to that first impossible climb that nearly killed me.

**It's time.**

I watched the clusters of pilgrims continue on their way. Students whom I had quickly walked around earlier, still laughing, still taking up the entire path. Pilgrims new to the trail nursing fresh blisters, their faces showing that special blend of pain and determination that everyone gets around day three. And some, like me, were weathered but committed, and had been walking long enough to form opinions about which brand of blister bandages was superior.

It was time for them. And it was time for me. The journey was releasing us, letting us go, sending us back into the world we'd left behind. The Camino had given us what it was going to give. Now we had to figure out what to do with it. I looked at the surrounding landscape. Tall eucalyptus trees stood like soldiers saluting the passing throng of pilgrims. This dreamy place, which awakened my senses, allowed my mind to wander, and filled my lungs with laughter, was letting me go. I was leaning against a mossy stone wall and let my fingers run along the soft green patches.

*The Camino is releasing you.* The words settled into my chest, quiet but undeniable. I could feel it—actually feel it—this sense of being let go. Not all at once, but like a slow exhale I didn't know I'd been holding. The tightness in my shoulders, the constant forward momentum that had carried me for weeks, all of it was softening. The path was loosening its grip.

I was about to close my eyes and take in one last inhale of the forest trail when a line of teenagers bumped into my backpack and bumped me back to reality. *Fiiiinneee. I'm going.*

I joined back into the current of walkers and tried to come to terms with the fact that I was nearing the end of my pilgrimage. In a day, I would walk into Santiago de Compostela, would stand in the plaza in front of that massive cathedral, would look up at those ancient spires and know that this journey was done.

Whether or not I was ready.

*19*

# Amatam

I sat on the edge of my bed, peeling off the last of the previous day's tape and bandages from my feet. Dirty, battered, covered in fresh calluses and half-healed blisters—they'd seen better days. *Gosh, these look terrible.* Each morning for the past forty-one days I had attended to blisters, lost toenails, calluses and cuts, but this was my last morning on the trail.

I flexed my toes experimentally. My right foot responded with a dull ache that radiated from heel to arch—a pain so familiar now that it felt almost friendly. My knee was tight and resisted my morning stretches.

Kathrine, already dressed, sat on her bunk and stared at her pack, seemingly unable to recall how to close it. We'd done this forty-one times, but somehow this morning felt different. Heavier. Like our bodies knew something our minds hadn't fully accepted yet.

We exchanged a look—no words were necessary. After six weeks of walking together, we'd developed our own language of glances and nods.

We made our way down to the small courtyard of the albergue after grabbing some coffee at the bar. The fog was thick, wrapping around everything like a soft blanket, muffling the sounds of the waking city. Kathrine and I sat in cold metal cafe chairs, warming our hands on our cups, neither of us saying much.

What was there to say? We'd traveled 800 kilometers to get here. We were less than ten kilometers from the cathedral. In a few hours, it would all be over.

I took a sip of coffee and watched the fog swirl. Since we weren't far outside of Santiago, we didn't mind the limited visibility. We had time. For once, we actually had time.

*This is it.*

The path unfolded before us one last time—more eucalyptus trees and mossy stone walls lining our way as we neared the edge of the city, their ancient surfaces slick with moisture. The scent of eucalyptus mixed with damp earth—a smell I'd become so familiar with over these few days that I knew I'd miss it. By the time we reached the edge of the city, the sun had broken through, burning off the fog. It warmed our shoulders, and I felt my body relax into the rhythm of walking one more time. *Left foot, right foot, breathe.* The simplest thing in the world, and somehow the most profound.

Somewhere along those final kilometers, we'd merged with our friends—Blake and Becky from Canada, and Gary from Australia. The five of us walked together, our boots finding an easy rhythm on the cobblestones. The path widened as we neared the edge of the city, and the landscape shifted. Rural gave way to suburban, then urban. Houses pressed closer together. Cars appeared on nearby roads. The sounds changed— less birdsong, more traffic, voices, city life humming in the distance.

Laughter bubbled up between us as we swapped stories, but there was an undercurrent of anticipation running through all of us. We were close. So close.

The cobblestones beneath our feet became more uniform, more polished. We were walking through actual streets now, past cafes and shops, past locals going about their daily routines.

My heart started beating faster. Not from exertion—we weren't walking that quickly—but from something else. Anticipation. Fear. Excitement. I couldn't quite name it.

The buildings grew taller, older. The street began to climb. And then I heard it—the faint sound of bagpipes floating over the noise of the city.

We rounded a corner, descended a final set of stone steps, and then—

The square opened up before us.

I stopped walking. Couldn't have kept moving if I'd wanted to.

The Catedral de Santiago de Compostela rose into the sky like something out of a dream. Massive. Ancient. Impossibly grand. Its twin spires punched through the blue, their Gothic peaks sharp against the soft clouds. The facade was a riot of carved stone—saints and angels and symbols I couldn't name, all weathered by centuries of wind and rain and the prayers of millions of pilgrims who had stood exactly where I was standing now.

I'd seen pictures. I'd studied the architecture. I'd imagined this moment for months.

None of it had prepared me for the actual sight of it.

The square teemed with pilgrims. Some stood in clusters, hugging, crying, laughing. Others lay sprawled on the cobblestones, their packs beside them, too exhausted or overwhelmed to do anything but exist in this space. A few knelt.

*We're here. We're actually here.*

My mind went into overdrive, the same way it had at Cruz de Ferro.

*What am I feeling, what am I feeling, what am I feeling?!*

*Just slow down. Breathe.*

*Am I crying?*

I was. Not choking sobs, but a steady stream of tears coating my cheeks, warm and unstoppable. I didn't bother wiping them away. What was the point? Everyone around me was doing the same thing.

I looked up at the cathedral again. The stone seemed to glow in the morning light, warm and golden and patient. It had been here for almost a thousand years. It had watched millions of pilgrims arrive, just like this, with tears streaming down their faces and blisters on their feet, and their hearts cracked wide open.

It would be here long after we left.

But right now, in this moment, it felt like it was here just for us.

I let my backpack slide off my shoulders. It hit the ground with a satisfying thud—the sound of completion, of finally being able to set the weight down.

Kathrine did the same, and then we were hugging each other, holding on tight, both of us crying and laughing at the same time.

*We did it.*

I pulled back and looked at my friends—Blake and Becky with their arms around each other, Gary standing with his hands on his hips, staring up at the cathedral like he was trying to memorize every detail.

*We did it.*

The next several minutes were a blur of pictures, hugs, and more tears. My eyes kept going from my friends back to the cathedral, checking to make sure it was actually there. Eventually, we made our way to the pilgrims office to get our Compostelas—our certificates of completion. The line snaked out the door and down the street. Pilgrims stood shoulder to shoulder, their faces showing various stages of emotion—some still tearful, some grinning ear to ear, some looking slightly dazed, like they couldn't quite believe they'd made it.

I pulled out my credential while we waited—that worn, stamped passport that had traveled with me from Saint Jean Pied-de-Port. The pages were soft from being handled, creased from being folded and unfolded, stained with coffee and rain and whatever else I'd subjected it to over the past six weeks.

I flipped through it slowly. Each stamp was a memory. The albergue in Roncesvalles where I'd collapsed after that first impossible climb. The musical meal with Gregorio. The ancient church where I'd lit a candle. The bar where I ate an entire plate of bacon.

Forty-one days of stamps. Forty-one days of walking. All leading to this.

The attendant called me forward, and I handed over my credential. He flipped through the pages with practiced efficiency, checking dates, making sure I'd walked the minimum required distance.

He nodded, satisfied, and reached for a blank Compostela certificate. His pen moved across the page in flowing script, filling in my name in Latin: "Amatam Wiseman."

I watched him write, mesmerized. There was something deeply satisfying about seeing my name in Latin, about this ancient ritual being performed the same way it had been for centuries.

He handed me the Compostela and my certificate of distance, both rolled and placed in a protective case, then offered me a warm smile of congratulations.

I stepped outside, holding the scrolls carefully. Kathrine joined me, her own Compostela clutched in her hands like it might disappear if she loosened her grip.

I unrolled mine, and we both stared at it. The ornate border. The official seal. A Latin text certifying that I, *Amatam Wiseman*, had walked the Camino de Santiago and arrived at the tomb of the Apostle.

The image of Spain's patron saint looked up at me from the page.

*I walked across Spain.*

It still didn't feel real.

The walk to our albergue was quiet. Our host was a sweet Italian man who greeted us with the kind of warmth that made you feel like family. We dropped our bags in the room and I collapsed onto my bunk, expecting sleep to take me immediately.

But I didn't sleep. I lay there with my eyes wide open, staring at the ceiling. *That's it. We're done.*

I shifted, trying to find a comfortable position. The deep, bone-tired ache in my body, which had been my constant companion for the last six weeks, felt so familiar it was almost like home. My feet throbbed. My knees protested every movement. But for the first time in forty-one days, I didn't have to walk tomorrow.

*I could sleep in. I could rest. I could do absolutely nothing if I wanted to.*

The thought should have been comforting.

Instead, it felt terrifying.

*What do I do now? Who am I if I'm not walking?*

For six weeks, my identity had been simple: I was a pilgrim. I walked. Every morning I woke up, put on my boots, picked up my pack, and walked. There was a clarity to it, a purpose. One foot in front of the other. Follow the yellow arrows. Find the next albergue. Repeat.

I rolled onto my side and stared at my yellow backpack slumped against the wall. It looked as tired as I felt, its straps worn, its fabric stained with sweat and dirt and who knows what else. We'd been through a lot together, that pack and me.

*What happens to you now? Do you just sit in a closet somewhere, gathering dust? A relic of a journey that's over?*

*What happens to me?*

I closed my eyes and tried to quiet the thoughts, but every time I did, I saw the trail stretching out before me. Felt the rhythm of my boots on the path. Heard the morning sounds of pilgrims packing up their things—the rustle of sleeping bags, the clink of water bottles, the soft murmur of voices preparing for another day of walking.

*It's over*, I told myself firmly. *You're done. You can rest now.*

But I didn't want to rest.

I wanted to keep on walking.

My thoughts didn't really move beyond that. We met up with Blake, Becky, and Gary later that evening at a cafe near the cathedral. They were already there when we arrived, sitting at an outdoor table with beers in hand. Stories we'd already told each other got retold and somehow got funnier.

The conversation flowed like wine, and the wine flowed generously. Our night out became something of a bar crawl. We toasted to the Camino, to our blisters, to terrible albergues and beautiful sunrises and the strange magic of walking hundreds of kilometers with strangers who became family.

With the evening carrying on and us moving from place to place, I felt a lessening of the tightness in my chest. The laughter helped. The company helped. Maybe this was okay. Maybe it could just feel like this—like sitting with friends, holding onto the journey for a little while longer before we all went our separate ways. While some were planning on celebrating til the morning, I was ready to call it a night.

The morning light found me at what would become my breakfast spot for the next few days—a little cafe just down the street from where I was staying. The best chai latte I'd ever had, made with soy milk. Gluten-free, vegan, and dairy free options everywhere. *Where has this place been for the last 800 kilometers?*

I dined alone, which I actually didn't mind. The cafe provided a nice, brief separation from the touristy air that had descended on Santiago—a quiet space to process everything that had just happened. The city felt different from the rest of the Camino, more polished, more crowded. As I suppose it's meant to be. It's the end.

Between sips of my chai, I people-watched through the window. I had bought new clothes earlier that morning—it was a thought that had gotten me through the hot, sweaty, tired hours of my final walking days. Now I sat there watching other pilgrims shuffle past in their dusty boots and sun-faded shirts. *Would they recognize me as one of them in my clean clothes and new sneakers?* Probably. The locals certainly could— they knew a pilgrim when they saw one, new clothes or not.

I wasn't ashamed of looking like a pilgrim, but shedding that skin felt both necessary and too quick. The reality was setting in: once I got on the plane for Dublin, I would shift to tourist status, then back to local. Unemployed, penniless local. *Living the dream.*

But first, there was Finisterre. Since our arrival in Santiago, the idea had been quietly growing: the Camino felt not quite finished. Santiago was the official end, the destination on every map and every pilgrim's lips, but Finisterre was something else. The edge of the world. The place where pilgrims had walked for centuries to watch the sun sink into the Atlantic and, sometimes, to burn their boots in a kind of ultimate release.

*I need to go to the end,* I thought. *All the way to the end.*

I was keeping my boots, though.

# 20

# Living on the Edge

The bus the following day wound along the coast, and I leaned my face to the window as the Atlantic appeared between hills. After weeks of dusty inland paths, the coastal air felt like a gift—crisp and clean and salty, so different from the plains we'd crossed. The landscape shifted from the rolling greens of Galicia to something wilder, more dramatic. Rocky cliffs dropped away to churning water, and the sky seemed bigger somehow, stretched wide and endless over the sea.

I had decided there were four steps I needed to take to complete my Camino: reach Santiago de Compostela, go to Finisterre, go to Mass, and get a tattoo. Because apparently walking 800 kilometers wasn't quite enough commitment.

Finisterre was smaller than I'd expected—a cluster of white buildings hugging the harbor, fishing boats bobbing in the water, the smell of salt and seaweed heavy in the air. This wasn't the polished tourist town that Santiago had become. This was a working village that just sat at what ancient people believed was the edge of the world.

James and Leo were waiting for us when we arrived. We spent the day wandering the town with no particular destination in mind. After weeks of having a logical goal—walk here, get there, arrive by this time— the freedom of aimless wandering felt both luxurious and slightly unsettling.

The streets were narrow and winding, lined with small shops selling postcards and shells and other pilgrim paraphernalia. Leo, Kathrine and I treated ourselves to gelato before making our way to the beach. We all rolled up our pants and waded into the gentle tide. I don't know how much time we spent on that shore, but we collected shells, climbed some boulders and let our feet relax in the cool, salty water.

We eventually found ourselves at a restaurant overlooking the harbor, settling into a table on the outdoor patio. The view stretched out before us—water and sky meeting at a line so crisp it looked drawn.

The waitress brought our food and a jug or two (or three) of sangria before closing the restaurant for *siesta*. She told us to hang out as long as we wanted. We ate slowly, savoring it, none of us in any hurry. The conversation flowed easily, the way it does with people you've walked hundreds of kilometers with. Stories we'd already told got retold with additional details. Moments we'd shared got examined from different angles.

Leo launched into story after story of all the people he connected with and recounted with fondness the day we chased a sunset in Castrojeriz. James talked about getting Covid and trying to navigate safely, distancing himself, taking care of his son, and recovering. Our Camino family had really stepped up looking after Leo, giving James time to heal and ultimately keep going. They had stayed well connected with everyone in our group and even got to meet up with Dan in Santiago.

Kathrine and I shared the egg incident, which had James and Leo both in tears from laughing. The way we told it now, it was hilarious—absurd and ridiculous—the horror of it had faded, leaving only the comedy.

The sun was sinking toward the horizon when we finally left the restaurant. The light had turned golden-orange, painting everything in warm tones. We sauntered back toward the bus station, none of us wanting this day to end.

When we reached the station, we stood in an awkward cluster, no one quite ready to say the words that needed to be said.

The silence stretched out, filled with everything we weren't saying. *Thank you for walking with me. Thank you for the laughter and the companionship, and for being exactly who I needed when I needed it. Thank you for becoming family in the space of six weeks.*

I stared at the bus like it had personally wronged me. Out of all the buses I had ridden, this was the one I was most reluctant to board. Aside from Kathrine, James and Leo were the pilgrims I had grown closest to, and I was more than tempted to follow them home to Australia—even if that meant excessive credit card debt and learning to cope with massive spiders.

We said our goodbyes—hugs all around, promises to stay in touch that we might or might not keep, attempts at casual cheerfulness that fooled exactly no one.

Kathrine and I climbed onto the bus, and the moment we sat down, we both turned in our seats, pressing our faces to the large window. James and Leo stood on the sidewalk, waving.

And then—I don't know who started it—they began to dance.

They were absolutely committed to it, performing with the kind of theatrical seriousness that made it even funnier. Other people waiting at the bus stop were staring at them like they'd lost their minds, which only seemed to encourage them.

Kathrine and I were laughing and crying at the same time, waving frantically through the window. The bus driver started the engine, and the vehicle rumbled to life beneath us.

We watched them until we couldn't see them anymore, until they were just two tiny figures in the distance, still waving, still committed to sending us off with joy instead of sadness.

I turned back in my seat and wiped my eyes. My cheeks hurt from smiling.

The next day in Santiago, we attended Mass at the Catedral de Santiago, an experience I was unprepared for. We'd arrived an hour early, and it was a good thing we did—the cathedral was already filling up. I joined the line of worshipers waiting to walk by the tomb of St. James and gave him a whispered, "Thank you", as I passed.

We found seats near the front and settled in to wait. The Mass took place in Spanish, and I understood maybe one word in ten, but it didn't matter. There was a language here that transcended words—the ritual of it, the rhythm, the collective breath of hundreds of people all focused on the same thing.

And then, toward the end, the moment everyone was waiting for: the *botafumeiro*.

Eight men in red robes emerged from the shadows and surrounded a thick rope attached to the large incense burner. The priest blessed the botafumeiro, and then—with a coordinated pull that must have taken years to perfect—the botafumeiro began to swing

Slowly at first, just a gentle arc back and forth. Then faster. Higher. The silver burner swung in great sweeping arcs across the transept, nearly touching the ceiling at the top of its swing. Smoke poured from it, thick and fragrant, filling the entire cathedral with the scent of incense.

It was mesmerizing. The flash of silver cutting through the air. The coordinated effort of the men pulling the ropes. The whooshing sound it made as it passed overhead. I considered recording it on my phone, but decided against it. This was a parting blessing, not a spectacle.

When we completed the fourth and final step the next day, the permanence felt right. I got a tattoo of a shell framed by olive branches on my back—simple, permanent, mine. Kathrine got the route line of the Camino on her arm. Our talented artist was hilarious and easygoing, keeping us laughing throughout the entire session. (Without messing up the design!)

Sunday morning found me back at the cafe one last time, spending far too much on breakfast and pretending to write in my blue floral notebook. People packed the small corner space—understandably, since it was Sunday and most other local establishments were closed. I was leaving for Dublin that afternoon, and the finality of it was starting to sink in.

I had said goodbye to Kathrine early that morning in front of the albergue. We sat quietly on a bench waiting for her taxi to take her to the airport.

"Well," Kathrine said finally, her voice tight.

"Well," I echoed.

And then we were hugging, and I was crying, and she was crying, and we were both laughing at ourselves for crying. We'd only known each other for six weeks. Six weeks. But we'd walked 800 kilometers together. We'd shared bunks and blisters and terrible hostel showers. We'd walked through pain and beauty and transcendence.

Kathrine had seen me at my best and my worst. She knew me in a way that very few people did, not because we'd shared deep secrets or had profound conversations, but because we'd simply walked together. Day after day. Mile after mile.

Later that morning, sitting in the cafe with my orange juice and chocolate con churros, I felt the weight of that goodbye settling over me. I really was leaving. The Camino was really over. Santiago was becoming just another city I'd visited once.

*I need to start budgeting for a juicer,* I thought, taking another sip of the orange juice. *Seriously, my children's children will hear about this orange juice.*

I pulled out my blue notebook and stared at the blank page, pen poised. *I should write something profound,* I thought. Something about what the Camino meant, what I'd learned, who I'd become. My flight wasn't for a few hours, so I had time to kill.

But the words wouldn't come. Maybe it was too soon. Maybe I needed distance before I could make sense of it. Maybe words couldn't capture some things at all.

I knew I would never walk the same again. Literally—my knee and feet would probably never be the same. But I hoped I would never forget the feeling I had right then, sitting between one life and the next, my battered backpack at my feet like an old friend.

Homesick for friends I'd only known for weeks. Excited for whatever came next. A little bit proud of myself too, if I was being honest.

Dublin felt like the right ending, even if I felt slightly out of place with my weird tan lines and post-pilgrimage waddle. I do love Ireland. But the pace felt jarring— people rushing past, cars honking, the constant hum of urban life. I was a tourist now, staying at a B&B, ticking off the list: Trinity College, the Book of Kells, Dublin

Castle, St Stephen's Green, Ha'penny Bridge, Temple Bar.

*What am I doing?* I caught myself speed-walking between landmarks like I was racing for a bed. *There's no albergue to get to. No pilgrims to outpace.*

But I couldn't seem to slow down. Tourist mode meant covering ground, seeing things, and moving efficiently. It was the opposite of everything the Camino had taught me.

That's when something yellow caught my eye.

In the window of an outfitter, there was a full Camino de Santiago themed display. Mannequins dressed as pilgrims stood around blocks covered in blue and yellow shells. Backpacks with travel guides, walking poles, sunglasses, and water bottles, all nicely arranged like some kind of shrine. I stood there staring at it for a long moment.

*There's just no escaping it, I guess.*

The feeling stayed with me as I kept walking, and before I knew it, I was standing in front of Saint Patrick's Cathedral. The stone facade rose before me: ancient, imposing, and beautiful. I honestly don't know where to start with this church, but I needed it.

I needed the worn stone walls. I needed the stained glass. I needed the sanctuary.

I had been wrestling with the feeling of being both pilgrim and tourist, and there in that cathedral I was neither. My identity crisis was left at the door. Whether or not I would pick it up on my way out was entirely up to me, but at that moment, it didn't matter. Centuries of prayer, centuries of worship, and centuries of stumbling believers just trying to get it right surrounded me.

All along the church walls, etched in metal plaques, is the "Breastplate of Saint Patrick." A prayer about Christ being ever present—with me, behind me, before me.

I glanced down at my new sneakers—clean, stiff, unmarked by any trail. And there, next to mine, I noticed another pair. Worn, weathered, dusty from the road.
*We did it*

## *Epilogue*

# Grapes and Yogurt

It's been four years since I walked the Camino, and I need to tell you something: adjusting to life back home was harder than the actual pilgrimage.

Trying to slip back into "normal" life felt like putting on clothes that didn't fit—uncomfortable, restrictive, and kind of itchy.

Here's what I've learned: the Camino doesn't end when you get home. It repeats itself.

I had heard from other pilgrims that there were three stages of the Camino: the physical stage, the mental stage, and the spiritual stage, and that you would know when you reached each one. Those three stages I experienced in Spain came around again, only this time on Michigan soil instead of Spanish dirt. The physical stage: my body healing, adjusting from twenty-five kilometers a day to sitting at a desk. I had my knee checked out and found that I had a torn meniscus. Despite the miles I had put on it, I was able to avoid surgery and let it heal over time. The mental stage arrived three to four months later: the ache for thin places, the conviction I'd never find creative space like the Camino again. And finally, the spiritual stage: the surrender, the letting go, the discovery that God was already here.

But I almost missed it because I was too busy trying to recreate Spain.

I'd done this before, actually. During my semester abroad at Oxford, I stayed with lively host parents in Charlbury, a charming town in the Cotswolds. My hosts, who were avid birders, frequently spent weekends in Wales searching for species not present in their back garden. They were quite active and had a strict health regimen where every morning meant whole grain toast and an egg, or yogurt with grapes. They didn't have coffee in the house, so I'd have a cup of tea instead, sitting at the breakfast table next to the back door that opened into their garden. Colorful blooms. Birdhouses. A book of English birds left out for me to peruse while I sipped.

I loved those mornings. Really loved them. So when I came home, I promised myself I would have grapes, yogurt, and tea every morning to keep me connected to Oxford.

That didn't last.

American grapes tasted different. The tea wasn't quite right. And without the garden view and the bird book, and the sound of my host mother puttering in the kitchen, the whole ritual felt hollow, like I was playacting a scene from someone else's life.

I should have learned my lesson then. Should have understood that you can't bottle a sacred moment and expect it to keep. But apparently I'm a slow learner, because I needed to make the same mistake twice, on a much grander scale, before the pattern became clear.

When I got back from Spain, I didn't just try to recreate breakfast. I tried to recreate an entire way of being.

The Camino had been transformative—truly, deeply transformative. So naturally, I assumed that maintaining the transformation meant maintaining the form. Early morning walks. Simplified living. Long stretches of silence. All the external practices that had opened me up on the trail, transplanted wholesale into Michigan soil. Wake up early. Walk. Pray. Simplify.

But it felt forced, performative. I was chasing the container instead of the content.

The recognition didn't come all at once. It crept up on me over weeks of failed attempts to make Michigan feel like Spain. One morning I was forcing myself through another "Camino-style" prayer walk, mentally checking off the boxes: slow pace, check; silence, check; "openness to God", check; when I realized I was doing exactly what I'd criticized about my old busy life. I was performing spirituality instead of living it.

That's when I realized my mistake: I'd idolized the Camino.

The Camino had become my golden calf. It wasn't the act of walking itself, but the concept that true faith happened in *that* place. *That* was where God showed up most fully. *That* was the standard against which all other spiritual experiences would be measured and found wanting.

It was a sobering realization. Also, honestly, a relief. Because if the Camino was just a container—beautiful, yes, but ultimately just a container—then maybe the contents were available elsewhere too. Don't get me wrong, I loved it and would suggest it to anyone who asks (and several people who don't). But I'd unknowingly set it up as my deliverance when it had truly been a catalyst. I'd forgotten that God can show up anytime, anywhere. Even in Michigan.

The Camino didn't cure my restlessness. I'm still antsy, still ready to say yes at a moment's notice, still dreaming about the next adventure. Before, I was addicted to being busy. I said yes to every opportunity, every committee, every favor asked. I wore my exhaustion like a badge of honor.

The Camino didn't fix that—it just helped me see what it actually was. A wanderer's heart chasing destinations instead of a pilgrim's heart seeking God.

Now I'm learning—slowly, painfully learning—to pause before I answer. To ask not "Can I do this?" but "Is God asking me to do this?" There's a difference between being available and being discerning. The Camino taught me I could walk twenty-five kilometers in a day; coming home taught me that just because I can, doesn't mean I should.

What actually changed wasn't the restlessness itself — it was what I'd been building my life around.

The Camino stripped away everything I'd added to my faith, exposing what had actually been holding me up: the performance, the need to have the right answer for every theological question, the belief that God measured my worth by how indispensable I made myself.

What grew in the clearing? Prayer, honest instead of polished. Community, smaller, deeper, more intentional. Service, chosen carefully instead of compulsively. Scripture, read with a hunger I'd never quite felt before, lingering long enough to let something new break through. Sabbath, actual rest.

Transformation, I'm learning, isn't usually the big event you can point to. It's the million small yeses that follow it. The Camino cracked me open. Staying open is the work.

Creativity snuck back in alongside the spiritual practices — stories I'd abandoned mid-sentence, characters waiting for their worlds to be built, a reminder that creativity isn't a luxury but part of how we're made. The emptying had been generative all along. Which kept bringing me back to the question that haunted me in Burgos: *What is a pilgrimage, really?*

It's an intentional spiritual journey. And the journey, I've learned, is less about the miles you log than the yeses you say along the way. I have no idea what God has for me next, but when I turn around and look at the wild provision and gracious surprises of these past four years, I'm all in. My pilgrimage is far from over, and I haven't even left North America! The dusty Spanish trail has been traded for prayer walks at Riverside Park. The cathedrals in Spain opened a door I hadn't thought to knock on — other traditions, other expressions, other ways of practicing the same faith. I came home wanting to understand not what divides us but what we're all reaching toward. That wondering turned into study — church history, different liturgical traditions, voices I'd never thought to seek out — and what I found wasn't division so much as a family that had forgotten it was one.

The pilgrim road had widened in ways I hadn't expected. And somehow, in the middle of all that expansion, ordinary life was still waiting. I wanted a good, steady job with regular hours, and I have that now. Monday through Friday, nine to five. Actual weekends off. My twenty-two-year-old self would be horrified. My thirty-something self is thrilled. But the routine doesn't cure the restlessness—it just gives it direction.

This morning I wasn't thinking about Oxford at all. I was running late, grabbed what was in the fridge—fruit, yogurt, granola, the usual. I ate standing at the counter, scrolling through my phone, already mentally at work.

Then I bit into a grape.

It wasn't the taste that stopped me—American grapes still taste like American grapes. It was something else. A sense memory, maybe. The quality of the morning light. The quiet. And suddenly I was back at that table in Charlbury, the garden door open, the bird book splayed beside my teacup.

But here's the thing: I wasn't sad about the distance. I wasn't aching for what I'd lost.

I set down my phone and looked out the window—no English garden, just my neighbor's garage and a scraggly walnut tree. I finished my breakfast slowly, deliberately, the way I used to in Charlbury. The way I learned to on the Camino.

And I felt it. That presence. The same nearness I'd known in Oxford, the same quiet communion I'd experienced walking through Spanish villages at dawn.

It had been here all along. I'd just been too busy trying to recreate the old containers to notice God showing up in the new ones. Grace doesn't wait for you to arrive somewhere worthy of it.

I've always had a hard time relating to homebodies. I like where I live, but I cannot fathom not wanting to explore somewhere new. To me, it feels as vital as breathing. Maybe that's why the Camino felt so right. Movement with purpose, exploration with meaning. But here's what I'm slowly learning: the wanderer's heart and the pilgrim's heart aren't the same thing.

A wanderer is always chasing the next destination. A pilgrim is looking for God—and God is everywhere. Even here.

I don't want to say—or hear—that I *was* a pilgrim. I've been branded. (Literally) But this mark reminds me not that I was once on the pilgrim road, but that I still am.

I am a pilgrim now. And a pilgrim I'll stay.

Even when I'm standing still. Even when the thin places feel harder to find. Even when I'm genuinely trying to bloom where I'm planted.

The Camino taught me how to walk with intention. Now life is teaching me how to stand with it. But also—

a trip to New Zealand sounds incredible. Or Italy. Maybe Greece?

The restlessness hasn't gone anywhere. I've just learned its real name: *longing*. And longing, it turns out, can point you toward God just as surely as contentment can. I'm learning to live in the tension. To be present in this place, this job, this ordinary life—while keeping my heart open to wherever God might lead next.

The grapes still taste different here than they did in Oxford. The path looks different than it did in Spain. But the *presence*? That's the same.

And that's enough.

# Discussion Questions

→  Can you describe a moment of *ultreia* in your life? How did it make you feel? How did it affect you and others around you?

→  What fills you up or grounds you when life feels full and good? What do you reach for when it's hard? Are they the same thing — or different?

→  Early in the story, I shared that my motivational song seems to be "Can't Get Next to You" by The Temptations. What's yours?

→  My injury threatened to derail the whole journey — but it didn't, and I'm glad. Have you ever had an experience that started in struggle or disappointment but turned into something you're now grateful for?

→  Do you have a healing balm friend? How would you describe the connection you have together?

→  What moments have you unknowingly traded because you were comparing yourself to others or trying to keep pace with others?

→  Describe a time you have taken proximity for granted? How have you strived to be intentional about your friendships and relationships since?

→  What does resting look like to you?

→ Describe a time when you were tongue-tied about what you believe. Looking back on that situation, how have you grown since?

→ Have you ever engaged in an intentional spiritual practice — pilgrimage, liturgy, fasting, sabbath, or something else entirely? What drew you to it, and what did you find there?

# Acknowledgements

This book would not exist without Terry DeBoer, who pestered me — in the absolute best way — to turn a sermon into something more. He cheered me on, checked in, and eventually pulled me into the orbit of Word Weavers International, which changed everything. I cannot thank him enough for that nudge (and all the nudges that followed).

Speaking of Word Weavers, the West Michigan branch deserves its own round of applause. You read my work, told me the truth about it, and made me a more confident writer in the process. I'm grateful for this community, for the craft we get to wrestle with together, and for the stories you've trusted me with along the way.

Thank you to one of my favorite Aussies, James Sage—editor, beta reader, Camino Yoda, and friend. Somehow, across all those time zones, you've been one of the most constant voices in this process. You wear a lot of hats and wear them well.

To Emma Roorda and Jessica Castro: you had an almost unreasonable amount of enthusiasm for this project before I'd even finished it, and you hollered at me (in love) every time I thought about procrastinating. But more than that— prayer warriors, travel buddies, spiritual counsel, former roommates, chosen family— you are simply irreplaceable. Words fall a little short here, which is ironic given the circumstances. I love you both. I also hope this makes you cry. (Heehee.)

To my dad, Les: thank you for writing the foreword and for a lifetime of love and encouragement, even when my ideas have been, shall we say, ambitious. And to my mom, Lori: you covered every single step of my Camino in prayer, just as you've covered my whole life— and the faith you and dad have modeled is a gift I'm still unwrapping.

To my sisters, Jill and Kelly: thank you for listening, motivating, and absorbing every vent session like the absolute champions you are. People who dread being the middle child are a mystery to me — being sandwiched between you two is one of my favorite things about my life. (That, and spoiling your kids, obviously). To the family and friends who came along for this ride: thank you for being there, in whatever way you were. It meant more than you know.

To my church family: thank you for building something truly rare — a community of grace and hope that has become a haven for so many. Your example of obedience and service has shaped me more than you know, pushing me deeper in my faith and reminding me what it looks like to live it out. I am honored and grateful to be part of this ministry.

And finally, to my big Camino family—but especially Kathrine Rasmussen, nephew Leo, and the one and only Jedi Master James: you turned what could have been a long, hard walk into one of the most joyful, hilarious adventures of my life. I don't know when our paths will cross again, but I have no doubt it'll be an absolute riot. I'll be forever grateful for every one of you.

Buen Camino

# About the Author

Amy is a Canadian Michigander, writer,
and avid traveler.
With a background in creative writing and
years serving in youth and worship ministry,
she is passionate about creating honest
conversations around faith, mental health,
and spiritual practices.
*Antsy Pants* is her debut book.


amywisemanwrites@gmail.com